The Place Between "Amen" and "I've Got It!"

Why Some Receive Sooner Than Later

by
Russell Plilar

Insight Publishing Group
Tulsa Oklahoma

The Place Between
"Amen" and "I've Got It!"
Why Some Receive Sooner Than Later

Published by INSIGHT PUBLISHING GROUP
8801 S. Yale, Suite 410
Tulsa, Oklahoma 74137
918-493-1718

Unless otherwise indicated, all Scripture quotations are
taken from the King James Version of the Bible.

Scripture quotations marked AMP are taken from *The
Amplified Bible, Old Testament* copyright © 1965, 1987 by
Zondervan Corporation, Grand Rapids, Michigan. *New
Testament* copyright © 1958, 1987 by The Lockman
Foundation. Used by permission.

All Greek and Hebrew references are taken from
James Strong's Exhaustive Concordance.
Nashville: Abingdon, 1890

Cover design by Shawn Sturm

ISBN 1-930027-06-0
Library of Congress 00-101856
Printed in the United States of America.

Contents

Dedication

First, to my wife Barbara, of twenty-eight years who I have been married to and still very much in love with. She has taught me what it truly means to wait and be patient in the Lord, and allow Him to work in His timing and His season for my life.

To my parents, J. D. and Freda Plilar that introduced me to God, family, and church at a young age.

To my sister Sharon, who is so giving, and has a beautiful spirit and beautiful countenance.

To my three wonderful daughters, Christy, Cheri, and Michelle, whom I love dearly and have exemplified beauty beyond measure, talent that speaks for itself, and character that reaches toward humanity. This book I pass on to them as a guideline and a guidepost to help them attain all that the Lord has in store for them.

To my good friend in ministry, who had the "word of the Lord" at the right time in my life, that saved my life, Neva Lema. I love you and cherish your friendship.

To my mother and father-in-law who showed me integrity, perseverance, and a willingness to keep going on in the midst of all adversity.

To my staff of able, talented, patient, and extremely gifted individuals. You're the best.

To our assistant pastors who labor in prayer, teaching, and guiding right alongside of us in this endeavor.

To my pastors in El Paso who showed us from the beginning that "God Is On Your Side," and learn to think big, believe big, and expect big.

To my spiritual father in the Lord, Ralph Osborn. Thank you for introducing me to Christ and Phillipians 4:19. *"The Lord will supply all your need"* really has become real in this area.

To our church and congregation that is a shinning example to people of God pursuing their dreams with faith and patience.

To our wonderful friends in full-time ministry who constantly "root us on" and challenge us to come up higher.

To the many friends whom we have known over the years. Your prayers of intercession did not go unnoticed.

To all of you who not only read this book, but meditate upon the theme and content. Let this book capture your heart and become a part of your destiny. Let it help you pursue your dreams while on this wonderful journey called life.

Foreword

Co-pastoring with his wife Barbara in San Diego, Pastor Russell is building a strong governmental church with an emphasis on the nations. He's traveled extensively overseas preaching and teaching, and has raised up his people in a strong heritage of faith with a firm understanding of the Word and God's principles. Out of that ability comes this book. I am happy to recommend it to anyone standing in the place of faith, waiting for a promise, prophesy, or harvest to manifest.

Both Russell and his wife have been on my teaching staff at Spirit Life Bible College and have helped me pioneer it from its inception in 1992. They have been faithful friends, steadfast in battle, and true to God's plan, Word, and heart.

You will be ministered to and probably adjusted some by the truth, the candor, and exhortation herein.

Roberts Liardon
Roberts Liardon Ministries

Introduction

There is a literal place between our excited shouts of "Amen" and the time when we actually receive and enjoy the manifestation of what we are believing for. I'll say this statement many times throughout this book: If you don't understand this strategic position, it will become the place where many dreams are aborted and lives are disillusioned. This is the place where many people conclude that faith is a myth and the promises of God are unattainable. For some, it is the place between spiritual life and death.

I've written this book because of my heart for the body of Christ. I've divided it into two sections, Part One and Part Two. If you're in this place between "Amen" and "I've got it," you may be frustrated and on the brink of giving up. I want you to know that this "place" is never easy for anyone, no matter how seasoned a person may be in the things of God.

A medical physician will prescribe medication to soothe the pain until the physical circumstances in your body have time to heal. Sometimes we need some quick relief to strengthen us as we receive total healing. Thus, I have written Part One to serve as an antidote to soothe your anxious questions and to calm unnecessary fears. You may be feeling extremely frustrated and hopeless. Part One is a quick "pain antidote" to help get your life back in order and to restore your hope. Once you've settled the issues in Part One, then go on to Part Two where I discuss in more detail the heart issues of timing, character, and the abundant life.

PART ONE

Chapter 1
The Place Between "Amen" and "I've Got It!"

Pastor Haus spotted me walking through a crowded church hallway.

"Russell," he called, "could I speak with you for a moment?"

"Sure," I responded.

"Do you think you could get a company limousine this weekend? There's a guest speaker I'd like you to pick up. His name is Benny Hinn."

"Who's that?" I asked inquisitively.

"Oh, you've probably never heard of him. He's a minister from Canada who has only been ministering in America for the past few years."

"No problem. Just tell me when and where you want me to pick him up."

The year was 1977. My wife Barbara and I were faithfully attending Church on the Hill, a flourishing Assembly of God congregation in Vallejo, California. Ron Haus, the senior pastor, knew I worked for a major transportation company that sometimes allowed me to use their executive stretch limousines on the weekends. He thought it would be nice to welcome our guest evangelist with a limousine ride to the church. I didn't mind at all. In fact, I enjoyed "sowing" my time in the service of the Lord.

A few years earlier, I had read two books written by Dr. Oral Roberts called, *Seed Faith Living* and *A Daily Guide To Miracles*. They had revolutionized my life. Dr. Roberts taught about sowing your time, love and money as a seed and expecting a harvest in return. Consequently, when pastor Haus called and asked me to pick up our guest minister, I was more than happy to oblige since I was on the lookout for opportunities to "sow."

When the time came to escort Mr. Hinn from the hotel to the church, my wife and I arrived ready to serve. We had never heard this man speak before, but from our first introduction we could sense the anointing upon his life. Benny was an explosive, high-energy, upbeat individual. We didn't have an in-depth conversation with him or receive any dynamic prophecies, but we were honored to carry his belongings during his first visit to our church. We had an inner sense of destiny, knowing that God was working to prepare us for our future.

The Call of God

For several years, my wife and I had felt a call to full-time ministry. Before attending Church on the Hill, we were involved in a Baptist church when a missionary came and showed slides of his mission in Africa. I remember how my heart burned within me when the missionary asked for workers to help him on the field.

"I'm signing up right now," I said to my wife, "I know I'm called to the ministry. I can feel it!"

"Sit down and be quiet, Russell!" my wife responded wisely. She knew that I was extremely impetuous in those days. She understood that the call of God was upon our lives, but she also saw the need for tempering and character development.

Negative pressure was mounting on my job, and I wanted to get out of the transportation business in the worst way. I was constantly saying, "I want to go into the ministry," but what I really wanted to do was to run from the pressure of responsibility and maturity. God wanted to bring stability to my soul because I had a tendency to run from opportunity to opportunity when things got hard.

The call of God was upon us nonetheless. The Holy Spirit bore witness to it wherever we'd go. More than once, people approached us and said, "We know that you're pastors. Where is your church located? We see the call of God on your lives." I was anxious for God to put us into the ministry, but I had to first learn how to develop the fruit of patience and godly character so I could successfully navigate my way through what I call: *the place between "Amen" and "I've got it."*

The Blessings Of God's Favor

The late 1970s was a time of praying and sowing for us. It wasn't until 1980 that the firstfruits of our harvest finally began to show up. During that year, my employer, the Southern Pacific Transportation Company, otherwise known as SP Railroad, moved our family from San Francisco to Houston, Texas. It proved to be another appointment with destiny.

We began actively attending a small word of faith church in North Houston. While we were there, my life was greatly impacted by a guest speaker named Bob Buess. He had written a book called, *Favor, The Road to Success.* The Holy Spirit used him to open my eyes to the truth that we can pray for God's divine favor to come upon every area of our lives. After hearing Bob speak, I immediately began praying for supernatural favor on my job. It wasn't long until blessings of great favor from God began to fall upon my work situation.

One morning in 1983, I was asked to drive a load of 300 Wall Street Journals to a board of directors' meeting in Lake Jackson, Texas. On the way, I was praying in tongues and worshipping God when suddenly, the Holy Spirit spoke. "I'm going to connect you with one of the people you've been praying for favor with," He said.

At the end of this three day board of directors meeting, I was asked to drive the executive vice president of sales to the Houston airport so he could catch a plane back to San Francisco. Although I had never met the man before, he had asked for me by name. During our hour-and-a-half long drive, we got to know each other. I sensed an inward stirring that something good was about to happen.

"Where are you from?" he asked me.

"El Paso."

"That's interesting. We have a fellow in our El Paso office who is getting ready to retire. How would you like to go back there?"

"Wow! I would love to."

"I think you would be perfect for the job. Why don't you go home and talk it over with your family and call me back."

I was an account executive for the company. The position this man was offering me was a three-tier jump up the corporate ladder. It wasn't standard procedure to move someone from an entry level position directly into a regional management position.

This is definitely the supernatural favor of God, I thought.

After speaking with my wife, I decided to accept the position. It was a wise choice. Looking back now, I see how it brought my family another step closer to fulfilling the call of God that was upon our lives.

The Call To Bible School

After moving my family back to El Paso to manage the West Texas sales office, we began attending Abundant Living Faith Center pastored by Charles and Rochelle Nieman. We plugged in immediately and began serving in the church in any way we could. While we were there, we befriended a couple who had been students at Rhema, the world renowned Bible school in Tulsa, Oklahoma, founded by Kenneth E. Hagin. Someone had given us some teaching tapes by Brother Hagin and we had been blessed by them, but we didn't know much about his ministry.

"Oh, you've got to go with us to one of the Rhema seminars," our new friends said, "these meetings are wonderful!"

It didn't take much to persuade us. We ended up going to the Rhema Winter Bible Seminar in 1985. By the end of that week-long conference, we thought we had died and gone to heaven! The prophetic song of the Lord touched us deeply and the teaching anointing was powerful! After that meeting, Barbara and I knew beyond a shadow of a doubt that the Lord wanted us to enroll as students at Rhema, so we stepped out in faith and applied the following year.

The Unexpected Delay

When Rhema accepted our applications, we were overjoyed. Everything seemed to be falling into place. My company was preparing to merge with the Santa Fe Railroad, but the Interstate Commerce Commission turned the merger down. In order to try to get the merger to work, the two companies began to reduce personnel by offering early retirement packages and special severance offers. I was sure I was going to receive an early buyout. It was perfect! A severance package would allow me to concentrate on school and not have to maintain secular employment.

We were excited about pursuing the call of God and we told all our friends about our plans. They even threw us a going away party. The excitement quickly disappeared, however, when the window of opportunity didn't open for me as I had hoped.

My company did begin to offer severance packages to some, but I was overlooked. As the time approached for us to leave for Rhema, Barbara and

I began to feel uneasy inside. We knew we were supposed to go, but suddenly the timing didn't seem right. At the last moment, we backed out and some of our friends began to criticize us for it.

"We thought you were people of faith. Why didn't you go?" they asked.

We didn't understand the sudden uneasiness, but we knew enough about the leading of the Holy Spirit to put our plans on hold. We determined to stay in El Paso until we felt an inner release from God to go. During the wait, we continued to attend Abundant Living Faith Center faithfully and we served the Lord with all of our heart.

The Floodgates Suddenly Open

Shortly after putting our plans for Bible school on hold, my wife and two ladies from the church began to pray together. They were inspired to pray about the scripture in Exodus where Moses was leading the children of Israel out of bondage. God had told Moses that when they left Egypt, they would not go out empty-handed, but instead, they would go out loaded down with all of Egypt's gold and precious belongings. (See Exodus 3:20-22.)

After my wife and these two ladies began to intercede, a tremendous breakthrough came. Suddenly, the heavens opened and showers of blessing began to flood into our life!

One day in June of 1987, when I returned to my office after an important sales call, my secretary said, "The board of directors held an emergency meeting and decided that those in middle management positions can now take early severance buy-outs."

The buyout consisted of a year-and-a-half of wages — more than enough to get us through Bible school! I knew inwardly God's hand was moving on our behalf. I boldly stepped out and said, "I'm not looking back," and I took it.

My boss and I were the only ones in the Pacific Southwest region who took the severance package. Later, when the company was bought out by their largest competitor, many lost their positions. Nevertheless, God had delivered me. My family and I were now able to leave for Bible school with the gold!

That was not the end of God's blessings either. Soon the floodgates were open and God's provision began flooding into our lives from every direction. We had already reapplied to Rhema and had been accepted. In July of 1987, as we were making preparations to move to Tulsa for our first year of Bible school, another amazing event occurred.

My youngest daughter, Christy, who was thirteen at the time, was seeing an orthodontist because she needed braces on her teeth. The orthodontist she was seeing was a multi-millionaire who went on hunting expeditions to Africa several times a year. When he found out we were interested in studying the Word of God, he began to take a liking to our family. He had an interest in godly principles himself, so he encouraged us to come to his home and start a Bible study. We declined because we were already planning to go to Bible school. When we shared our plans with him, he showed immediate interest and wanted to know more.

As the time approached for us to leave, this man phoned me unexpectedly and said, "I heard you're leaving. I would like to take you to lunch before you go."

"Sure," I responded.

We met later that day at a restaurant across town. After a bit of light conversation, he asked me about our plans for Bible school.

"How much is it going to cost for you to go to school for these next two years?"

I told him that my company had given me a severance package and that we had plenty of money. It was true. When my wife and I began cashing everything in, we found that we had more than enough for the full two years.

"I want to pay your tuition for both years," he announced unexpectedly.

At that time, tuition was about $1600 a year, so that was about $3500 for me alone. I was amazed.

"You don't have to do that," I objected, "we're in good shape."

"I want to," he insisted.

I finally accepted and left the restaurant rejoicing in God's provision.

The following day, the two intercessors my wife had been praying with took her to lunch at the same restaurant. This orthodontist happened to see her sitting there so he went over and began talking with her.

"Are you going to enroll in Bible school with your husband?" he asked.

"Yes," my wife answered.

"Really? I didn't know that."

After talking with Barbara about a few other unrelated things, he went back to his office and called me.

"Russell, I didn't realize that Barbara was enrolling as a student with you. Her tuition needs to be paid too, right?"

"Yes," I answered.

"I'm going to call my bookkeeper right now and have him cut a couple checks and pay for her too!" God was doing exceedingly abundantly above all that we had asked or thought. We were walking in faith. We never asked people for money or mentioned our financial situation to anyone. We believed God and we never doubted. We just prayed and trusted God and the provision began to roll in miraculously. God was teaching us how to hold on to our faith in the place between "Amen" and "I've got it."

More Blessings From Heaven

The blessings just kept on coming. About the same time, our middle daughter, Michelle, who worked as a flight attendant for Continental Airlines, secured some discount passes for family members so we could visit some old friends in the San Francisco Bay area before flying off for Bible school.

As we were concluding our week-long visit in San Francisco, I said to my wife, "Let's go see Dr. Don before we leave." Dr. Don was a chiropractor friend of ours who had attended Church on the Hill with us back in the early '70s. He had been a friend of our family for many years. When I called him and told him we were in town and we were heading off to Rhema for two years, he wanted to see us immediately.

"I always wanted to go to Rhema," he said. "I'd like to buy you lunch today. Let's meet at the El Torito restaurant in Concord."

"Great!"

Later, as we were sitting in the restaurant sharing all the Lord had done for us, he unexpectedly asked, "How much is it going to cost for you to go through school?"

"Don," I said, "the tuition is already paid and the railroad gave me a severance buyout. Everything is already taken care of."

"Well, what about Christy, your daughter? She needs to be in school. That is going cost you quite a bit. My wife and I are making plans to build a house down on the water, in Benicia, California. While we were sitting here talking, the Holy Spirit impressed me to put that on hold and send you $500 a month for the next two years. He told me that if I would build His house, He'd build mine."

My wife and I looked at each other with absolute amazement.

Dr. Don did exactly what he said. For the next two years, checks came to us every month like clockwork. I remember him saying, "If I partner with someone else's vision, God will help fulfill my vision." He knew how to work the principles of God's kingdom.

Needless to say, we were blessed. When we finally left for Bible college, we were more excited than ever. The windows of heaven were open and God just kept right on pouring. When we arrived in Tulsa, God gave us a better house than anything we had when I was employed by the transportation company. The blessings just kept on coming and there seemed to be no end in sight.

The Place Between "Amen" and "I've Got It!"

Any experienced farmer knows that a harvest doesn't come overnight. There is a period of time that occurs between the time of sowing and the time of reaping. Barbara and I did a lot of praying and sowing in the late 1970s, but we didn't begin to see a return on our giving until the 1980s. There was a period of time that elapsed between the time we said, "Amen" and the time we said, "I've got it!" Actually, we didn't see the fullness of our "I've got it" until God supernaturally enabled us to become the pastors of a church that Barbara and I still pastor today. I describe the amazing details of that story at the end of this book.

In the following chapters, I will share the many principles God taught me as my wife and I waited in faith for the manifestation of God's blessings. I believe these truths will be a blessing to you as you undertake your own journey through the place between "Amen" and "I've got it."

Chapter 2
Time is On Your Side

"The Lord is good unto them that wait
for him, to the soul that seeketh him."
                                        Lamentations 3:25

Did you know that most people give to God —
"sow" their seed — on Sunday and expect a harvest
by Monday morning? It's true. It would be great if
Ed McMahon knocked on your door with a ten
million dollar check while you were reading this
book! But an immediate supply is not something that
happens every day. An instantaneous supply is
called a *miracle.*

Now I believe in miracles and look for them every
day. We know that God is a sovereign God, and He
can bring an immediate return on our giving. But as
believers, we need to know how to cooperate with
miracles and how to progress while we're waiting,
standing, and stretching for an answer!

In our fast-paced society, it's very hard to wait for
anything. We would feel cheated without the fast

food drive-through, the microwave oven, the ATM machine, the world-wide internet that instantly connects us with other nations, and hundreds of other modern conveniences. Unfortunately, we can be trained to set our desires and expectations in life based on the instant technology around us. But God has set a spiritual principle in motion, and we've just read it from the book of Lamentations. God is good to those who wait for Him.

You may be moaning, "Oh no, Pastor Russ! You mean I have to wait for something?"

Yes! Why? Because God wants to show His goodness to us as we seek Him.

We've all been in the difficult, and sometimes strange place, between "Amen" and "I've got it." Perhaps you're living in that place right now. It's easy to say "Amen" when you agree with something. But saying "Amen" and actually obtaining and possessing what you agree with are two different things.

You see, there's something between the moment when you sow your seed and the season of your harvest. There's something between the place where you are praying and believing, and the moment you actually obtain. That place has a name. It's called "time."

God's timing has nothing to do with earthly time. Earthly time has a predetermined hour, minute, and second. We wait for the hour when we get off work. We wait for our lunch hour. We wait for the hour of a scheduled meeting. We wait for the hour of a scheduled arrival or departure. We have conditioned ourselves in the natural realm to wait for the appointed time. Yet in the spirit realm, we find ourselves restless and discontent if we have to wait for God's answer longer than we expected.

Before we go any further, you need to understand that God's timing begins when it starts and ends when it's finished. God's timing comes in spiritual *seasons*. Sometimes in those seasons, every door is open to us; or every door seems shut.

There are certain timings where an opportunity must be taken within a certain season or it's gone forever. When that kind of timing comes, you'll be very aware of it.

In this book, we're going to discuss the time between sowing and the harvest. This particular time is usually hard on us in the natural, but if we can understand how to go through it and how to work with it, then we'll realize that this time is our friend.

If you are in this place of time, welcome! This is a very special place for you. It is filled with supernatural ingredients which will transform you into His image. Within this timing are the keys to the uncommon. Time is a wonderful place and it's imperative that you learn how to receive from it and wait in it.

You must also know that there are enemies who want to stop you from entering into the harvest. If those enemies can't stop you from sowing, they'll attempt to discourage you while waiting for the increase. This place between "Amen" and "I've got it" is also the area of their assignment. It is where the battle for your harvest begins.

The Lord intends for our harvest to come sooner than most of us see it manifest. What then, causes our harvest to come at a later time than God had planned? The answers reside in this particular and exciting place of time. In this place between "Amen" and "I've got it," we can think that we're just standing still, waiting for God to come through. But the truth is, during this entire time we're either advancing or retreating; birthing or aborting; maturing or stunting the outcome.

The difference between going on or stalling comes from the spiritual roadblocks that will always be standing in your way. It's up to you whether you will be stopped by them or hurdle over them.

I want to give you the keys to waiting. I want you to be able to go through every roadblock and hindrance that tries to detour you off course. I want to give you a spiritual boost as you hurdle. I believe that as you make the necessary adjustments, your harvest will be one that comes sooner instead of later. So let's get started.

Chapter 3
Roadblock #1: Criticism

If you're doing anything worthwhile, or if you're making any kind of progressive change for the better, people will criticize you. In fact, there are only three ways to avoid criticism: *do nothing, be nothing, and say nothing*. I know people who are diligently working to do all three.

Even Jesus said that if you are persecuted for His sake, to jump for joy because you have a great reward in heaven. (See Matthew 5:10-12.) But if you are the one guilty of causing persecution and speaking the criticism, then I believe we can reverse the meaning of that scripture. Small will be your reward in heaven — and little, if any, will be your reward on earth.

Criticism is a major roadblock in the place between "Amen" and "I've got it." Waiting can sometimes appear as a burden, so anger and agitation sets in. When people get aggravated, you can usually count on criticism to follow.

I've seen it happen time and time again. The scenario is always the same. It goes like this. Everyone around you is getting blessed, but you've given more than all of them. You've been a Christian longer, a faithful tither, and consistent in attendance and service. Yet they are all receiving their harvest, giving their praise reports, shouting, crying, and dancing while you sit there barely able to pay the monthly electric bill.

It's a set-up. Remember this: Just as no person's DNA is the same, neither is the time of their harvest. *Just as God has a unique calling upon your life, He has a unique timing for your harvest.* You must understand that everything around you is the same as before. You're just in a different spiritual time frame.

I'm reminded of a woman giving birth. When the contractions begin, everything is still wonderful. The bed is comfortable, she still sees her husband as a sweet lover and companion, and the moment rings with excitement and wonder.

But then the labor stage called "transition" hits. That same woman turns into Sybil, the woman with sixteen personalities. The contractions are unbearable. The bed feels like a rock. If the husband even looks her way, he's in serious trouble. Her moment of bliss has turned into an excruciating, hellish nightmare. And the funny thing about it all, is nothing in the room has changed. The husband is still the same, the nurses are the same, the room is still the same.

Nothing has changed but *her*. She's in a different time. She's in transition. She may be mad at everyone who touches her. She may be sorry she ever got in that condition. But one thing is for certain. She is going to reap what was sown. How she handles it will determine the joy of the moment.

We can use that natural analogy in the spirit realm. Remember how joyful and happy you were in the time of "Amen?" Well, everything around you is still the same. Nothing has changed outwardly or according to the Word of God.

However, you may be in a different time. You may now be in the place between "Amen" and "I've got it." So how you handle this time will also determine your joy and the timing of your harvest.

If you don't have a true revelation of that fact, then you'll become critical and murmur against God.

The "M" Word

Do you know what murmuring is? It's saying that what God has done for you isn't good enough. It's saying that He doesn't love you enough to take care of you, or see to it that all of your needs are met. It's placing yourself above God by thinking you can make better decisions than He can.

Sometimes we can actually come to the place where we don't know what else to do. That's not the time to become critical and murmur against God. The enemy would love to throw a net for you right here.

He wants you to become discouraged and moan, "I've done everything I know to do, and God's not doing anything. God's not going to help me. This stuff doesn't work." Don't fall for it.

It's true that you may have done all you know to do. But that simply means you need to know how to do more! I'm so glad that I realize I don't know it all. Wouldn't Christianity be boring if everything you knew was all there was to it? I shudder at the thought! We should be ever learning, growing, and changing from glory to glory.

God hasn't changed the plan and He didn't lie. He will do what He says. Maybe you need to understand more about Him. Maybe you need to get in the Word and learn more of His ways before you're so quick to murmur and become critical. Don't abort the seeds you've planted just because you don't understand how they grow.

In this place between seedtime and harvest, we must be very careful to guard against murmuring and criticism. A sharp, discontented tongue can quickly abort your harvest for a job, a mate, financial increase, or anything else you are believing for.

Take Heed How You Hear

Are people born critical? No!

Criticism begins with a thought. Every one of us has to guard against thoughts that will thwart our viewpoint, but I've noticed this especially with people who operate in some degree of the prophetic.

Prophetic people are gifted to see and observe the actions and words of others. But if they aren't mature, then what they see can turn into criticism and the results are overbearing and bitter. The inability to handle what they see with their gift can cause disastrous results. They never get to the harvest that's produced from building and planting. Instead, they only reap the rooting out and the tearing down because of a critical heart. We've seen so much of that style of ministry that sadly, many think it's the entirety of the prophetic.

Your thoughts are very private and only you and the Lord hear them. But just because they're private doesn't guarantee your safety. If critical, judgmental thoughts go unrestrained, they will soon affect you. What was once private is now on public display through your words and your actions. If we listen to the lies of the enemy, then our viewpoint becomes distorted. Thoughts can change your outlook, your personality, your ethics, your character — every part of your being can be affected positively or negatively by repeated thoughts.

It's War!

That's why the apostle Paul strongly instructed us in 2 Corinthians 10:5 to cast down imaginations, *"and every high thing that exalteth itself against the knowledge of God,"* and bring *"into captivity every thought to the obedience of Christ."* We are to bring unruly, critical thoughts under the obedience of Jesus Christ.

You might be wondering what it means to bring a thought under obedience to Jesus. Strong's Exhaustive Concordance defines "obedience" as attentive hearkening, compliance, and submission [#5218].

That means when an adverse, critical thought comes your way, the battle is on! It's the time for your spiritual antennas to go up, and to *attentively hearken* to the Word of God against the critical thoughts you're hearing. Although it may temporarily feel good to be critical, the good feeling will soon pass.

Before you know it, soulish poison spreads throughout your being and nothing feels good anymore. Everything goes wrong, everything seems wrong. Life is just miserable. And in the midst of feeling that way, someone comes along and preaches about a harvest. Every point the preacher makes, your mind will answer with a critical thought. If critical poison has spread throughout your soul, you won't be able to believe that a harvest will ever come to you.

I'm telling you that when criticism comes, pull out your biggest bombs. It's war! Hearken to the Word of God. Yield to His ways and His point of view. Only then will the battle be won and victory with peace will come.

Do you realize that pride is the number one cause for a mean, critical spirit?

You may respond, "No, Pastor Russ. I'm this way because someone betrayed me."

I would never be insensitive to hurt and betrayal, but we've all been hurt and we've all bled. The difference between the forgiving person and the critical person is *pride*. The thoughts of what others have done to you have never yielded or complied with the covenant of peace found in Jesus Christ alone.

It's True...We Reap What We Sow

"Do not judge and criticize and condemn others, so that you may not be judged and criticized and condemned yourselves.

For just as you judge and criticize and condemn others you will be judged and criticized and condemned, and in accordance with the measure you [use to] deal out to others it will be dealt out again to you."

Matthew 7:1-2 AMP

Who wants a harvest of bitter roots? Who wants to dig and plow in criticism only to reap pungent weeds? In this place between "Amen" and "I've got it," guard against criticism and condemning judgment. The enemy will make sure you have plenty of opportunity to become upset or dismayed. Instead, blast through that roadblock. Hurdle it, demolish it, whatever you have to do to make certain that criticism is put far from you. Begin to enter into your covenant of peace and a whole new way of life will come to you.

Chapter 4
Roadblock #2: Words of Doubt

Did you know that every temptation, every circumstance, and every challenge the devil brings is to make you doubt the Word of God? It's true. If he can make you doubt what God has spoken to you, then he's won that particular battle.

Doubt is a terrible thing. It swiftly paralyzes a person into a dazed-like lethargic state, and causes them to feel depressed, hopeless, rejected, angry, and bitter. In fact, I could go on and on listing the negative attributes doubt will cause in your life. You name it and doubt can open the door of your heart to it. You must always be feeding your faith and starving your doubts. If you don't learn how to combat the seeds of doubt, then you can doubt yourself, doubt others around you, and worst of all, doubt God.

Genesis 3 records the first entrance of doubt into the earth. God had given Adam and Eve His promise, telling them what He desired and what they were to do. Satan came to turn their wills away from the promise of God by planting seeds of doubt in their minds. You'd think Satan would try to use dramatics and wild antics to turn Adam and Eve from the glory of God to the darkness of his heinous depths. But he didn't. Satan tumbled them with one question — because that question gave entrance to doubt. He simply asked, *"Yea, hath God said...?" (Genesis 3:1).*

When Eve heard the question, she began to doubt herself. She wasn't exactly sure what God had said, so she rambled off something that sounded similar to what He meant. I can just see Satan smiling to himself when he heard her response. He knew he had her. Why? Because Eve didn't know what God had said. It wasn't in her heart.

So Satan challenged her memory. He probably coerced her confusion by saying something like, "No, God didn't say what you thought, Eve. You can eat anything you want and not die. Go ahead. Tell Adam. He probably misunderstood it too."

Satan had just thrown Eve a screaming curve ball called doubt, and she didn't hit it away. In fact, I don't think Adam and Eve even picked up the bat! So Satan succeeded by using doubt to cause Adam and Eve to miss out on their harvest.

Things haven't changed in our day. If anything, doubt is trying to increase and prevail as a way of life.

You must realize and know that doubt is a deadly killer in the place between "Amen" and "I've got it." When in this place, you must be very protective of what you've sown. Some people give sacrificially. Some feel led by God to give great amounts by faith. Doubt will swiftly destroy your seed, eating it like a cancer. It lurks in the shadows, watching and waiting for an opportunity to hit. It waits for a moment when you might feel down or discouraged.

Doubt waits for the time when friends speak unbelief to you. It waits for the time when your mate doesn't understand what's happening, and strife comes into your home. It waits for the time when you may not feel well in your body, when you're tired, or when the odds seem overwhelmingly against you.

Doubt knows that it will always have an opportunity to hit you. If you realize that, then you'll ground yourself in the Word of God and plant your feet firmly on the promises God has spoken to you. Doubt can only win when you're not ready for it.

Ouch! I've Been Hit!

How do you know when doubt hits you? You'll start wondering if you did the right thing. You'll start wondering if God will do the same for you as He did for others. You'll start listening to the opinions and fears of others. You'll start wondering if the call and plan of God will ever be fulfilled in your life. You may even begin to think that you're not worth

41

much, that you're going nowhere, or that you're living in a delusion.

If you're thinking those types of things, stop it — quick! Go back to the Word of God, find His promises, and stand on them. Allow the voice of the Word to rise above all the other muttering and echoes.

Ephesians 6:17 and Hebrews 4:12 tell us the Word of God is a sword to cut, divide, and annihilate the devil and the flesh from the spirit. So hit doubt where it hurts! Jab it with the sword of the Spirit — the Word of God. Refuse to speak fear. Refuse to waver in your opinion or become unsettled.

This isn't some "name it and claim it" doctrine. I'm not trying to make you feel better or encourage you through a "positive mental attitude." I'm declaring to you that the Word of God should be understood and written upon the very core of your being. The very power between life and death is found when we believe His Word. You can't base your faith — or the outcome — on some good message that was preached or on what your best friend did. Your actions must be based on the promises in the Word of God that have become a revelation to you. The corresponding action from what you believe is what produces a sure reward.

Faith in God is not a gamble. There is a risk involved that affects your mind and your flesh, but it's not a gambling risk. When people gamble, they hope to come out with more than what they put in. With God, if you read His word and allow it to become alive within you, then the reward is sure. As I've said before, there is a period where situations seem unsure. There is a place where you are no longer in control of the outcome or the timing of it.

A life without chances has no advances. That is the risk of where you abandon your care and solidly replace it with the promises found in the Word of God. That place is between "Amen" and "I've got it!"

In this highly spiritual place between your seed and harvest, the only strength you'll have to hurdle over the roadblock of doubt is the Word of God. Make sure to settle His promise within you, then allow that promise to grow to such strength that it literally changes the atmospheres you walk into. God doesn't intend for you to come up short or for your harvest to come later instead of sooner.

So right now, before you read the next chapter — if you don't have promises that are alive within you, go to the Word of God and find them. Read them over and over. Think about them throughout the day. Mediate upon them at night when you lay down to sleep. Then when those promises become an absolute revelation to you, blast the curse of doubt from your pathway! You will reap what you sow, and your harvest will not be stunted or stifled!

Chapter 5
Roadblock #3: Walking Backwards

"And Jesus said unto him, No man having put his hand to the plough, and looking back, is fit for the kingdom of God."
Luke 9:62

I don't know of any farmer who has successfully plowed his field while looking backwards. In the old days, it took great strength to push a plow and keep it on course. Can you imagine if the farmer tried to look backwards? First of all, he wouldn't be looking ahead, so how could he see where the plow was going? The rows would be crazy and zigzagged. The plow wouldn't make much of an indentation in the field. Secondly, the farmer wouldn't have strength moving forward, while at the same time, turning around to look behind him. Try it for yourself!

I want you to understand that looking or walking backwards will rob you of the strength it takes to get from "Amen" to the place of "I've got it!" Here's why.

The word "fit" in the Strong's Concordance [#2111] is interpreted in the Greek as well-placed. However, this word is derived from another Greek word [#5087] meaning in a passive or horizontal posture.

If you are in the place between "Amen" and "I've got it," yet are constantly looking back into your past, constantly rehearsing what has happened instead of what will happen, then you've placed yourself in a passive and lethargic position. If you are basing your future on everything around you — looking horizontally instead of vertically to God — then you're probably weak-willed, depressed, and intimidated.

How can you ever plow into the unknown and take what is rightfully yours when you're too busy comparing yourself to another, or worried about what someone else is saying about you? How can you ever trust God for your future if you're still looking horizontally — scared of the outcome because of hurts in your past?

Forward, Ho!

God wants you to walk forward because that's where the blessings are. Look at His promises in Jeremiah.

> *"But this thing commanded I them, saying, Obey my voice and I will be your God, and ye shall be my people: and walk ye in all the ways that I have commanded you, that it may be well unto you.*

> *But they hearkened not, nor inclined*
> *their ear, but walked in the counsels and*
> *in the imagination of their evil heart, and*
> *went backward, and not forward."*
> Jeremiah 7:23-24

Walking forward means to progress towards the mark or the goal of our high calling. When we listen to and obey God's instructions, we will walk forward. According to Jeremiah, it's only when we listen to and obey our own reasoning and imaginations that we go backwards.

The Bible states in 1 Corinthians 13:12 that right now, we see through a glass darkly. The Amplified version of that same verse says that our spiritual vision is somewhat blurred. In other words, we can't see the entire picture as God sees it. Our outlook and our viewpoint are limited, so why would we want to reason out and attempt to orchestrate our future?

Look straight ahead and follow the voice of the Lord. Leave your past behind. If God tells you to do something, shut down your fleshly imaginations and carnal reasoning. Obey the Lord and walk forward into your destiny.

I think of the early settlers venturing towards America. They left everything that was familiar to them. Everything they had come to be dependent upon was left behind. All they could do was look ahead and trust the Lord for the outcome. Any pioneer has done the same. They learn from their past but they don't stand around waiting for it to happen again. They are moving forward, plowing ahead, and always believing that the best is yet to come.

Don't sit around until you die. If you don't like the way things are happening around you, then listen to the Lord, get up, and move forward!

Patience and Endurance

> *"Do not, therefore, fling away your fearless confidence, for it carries a great and glorious compensation of reward.*
> *For you have need of steadfast patience and endurance, so that you may perform and fully accomplish the will of God, and thus receive and carry away [and enjoy to the full] what is promised."*
> *Hebrews 10:35-36*

Patience and endurance not only cause us to hurdle spiritual roadblocks and to fully accomplish the will of God, but they enable us to receive and carry away — as our possession — that which was promised. Do you understand that? Patience and endurance will carry you from the "Amen" into the "I've got it!"

Those verses don't say that after we have done the will of God we can go home and not go to church anymore. It doesn't say that after we've done our part we can send the wives in our place. No. God says we need endurance, persistence, and perseverance, and we can only have that by doing it. Even after we are promoted, God intends for us to continue in our pursuit of Him. But too many times when we are promoted, God gets demoted in our lives.

"God, I need a thousand dollars. I need it quick."

God says, "Will you worship Me?"

"Well, God, I'll send my wife. I'm really busy — remember the promotion I got? My home has been a disaster, my kids are acting wild, and I'm just really busy, so I won't be at church for a while." God becomes demoted by the promotion that He gave you.

Don't live that scenario. Continue to patiently endure until the set time has come for you. Don't stop at one blessing. Persevere into the full harvest for your life. To follow God means you must be moving ahead. You can't follow something backwards. Move forward. Be disciplined. Don't just hear the Word of God — become a disciple of it.

Determine that at any cost, you will not look to the left or the right, but instead will look vertically to Jesus, the author and finisher of your faith — and your harvest!

Chapter 6
Roadblock #4:
Disobedience

*O*bedience will always precede the manifestation.

The Lord gives us specific instructions in Isaiah 1:19, *"If ye be willing and obedient, ye shall eat the good of the land."* The Living Translation of the same verse says that if we will listen to the Lord, if we allow Him to help us, then He will make us rich. That's why God gave us two ears and one mouth. He expects us to listen twice as much as we talk. We will receive blessings when we listen.

Deuteronomy 28:2 says, *"And all these blessings shall come on thee, and overtake thee, if thou shalt go to Rhema Bible Training Center; get your Master's degree from Oral Roberts University; then go to another Bible school; obtain a doctorate, or the equivalent."*

No! The Bible doesn't say that. I inserted it to get your attention and cause you to consider if you have any wrong thinking. I'm for these schools and I support them. I love Bible schools! I teach in Bible schools! Although I'm a Rhema graduate, that's not what makes me blessed. My Rhema diploma doesn't cause me to enter the Promised Land and take what is rightfully mine. Sadly, some don't believe you're qualified to be a leader or qualified to receive the blessings unless you've graduated from Bible school.

But what does God have to say about that? He's the One who is with you in the place between "Amen" and "I've got it." He's the One who will instruct you on the obedience you need for your personal life. Let's read the scripture again without my personal sidetrack.

> "And all these blessings shall come on thee, and overtake thee, if thou shalt hearken unto the voice of the Lord thy God."
>
> Deuteronomy 28:2

God made it very simple with His instructions to us. He said that blessings would come upon us and overtake us if we would obey His voice. End of discussion.

God Can't Work With "Stupid!"

Once, in a minister's meeting, Dr. Lester Sumrall abruptly stated, "God doesn't respond to stupid!" God doesn't respond to it, nor does He talk it. So while you're in this place of timing, God is not going to tell you something stupid. He's not going to tell you that the first person who walks in with a red dress is your new wife. He won't tell you to jump off a building and cause you to walk on air so others can see a miracle. He won't tell you to go stand on the freeway and the first person who pulls over has a personal word from God for you. No. God will primarily speak to you through His word. We are to read and be watchful concerning the truths in the Word.

Often while you are in this place of timing, you may read a certain scripture and it will become illuminated to you or stand out from the other scriptures. That is God speaking to you through His Word. From that certain scripture, you may realize that you need to do something in particular. The very action you take may be what is necessary to help you get through this time of waiting for the harvest.

But some Christians get impatient. They don't know how to allow obedience through the Word to strengthen their patience, so they search for an immediate relief or some sort of action. They want to call a psychic to see what the occult has to say. They want to write Ann Landers and get her opinion. They want to call everyone and their mother to get other opinions. They watch those slimy talk shows and hear how Mikey turned into a woman because he couldn't get any answers in life. They become more frustrated and confused.

Some go on excessive shopping trips and partake in other indulgences, trying to escape the pressure of waiting for the timing of God. Then they find themselves in more trouble than they started with.

It seems that impatient believers go everywhere else but to the Word of God. The problem with many Christians is they spend money they don't have and buy things they don't need to impress people they don't even like.

Obedience is so important. It fuels endurance, patience, and persistence. While in the place between "Amen" and "I've got it," the wait can seem extremely long if we're not watching over the Word, studying it, and making it alive in our lives. If we don't give diligence to what the Word is speaking to us, we can be tempted into disobedience and eventually, give up on our harvest.

We need to constantly remind ourselves that even though we may not be seeing anything happen in the natural, the spirit realm is always active and moving on our behalf. When the harvest manifests, how do you think it got here? Do you think it just exploded out of nowhere? No! God was working in the spirit realm all the time that you thought nothing was happening.

The Ultimate Steward

In the place between "Amen" and "I've got it," there are a variety of things happening. We know the enemy is there to abort or stunt our harvest. But God is also there, proving us so we may handle our harvest.

You may argue, "Well, Pastor Russ, I didn't think that God would test me!"

Think again. God knows exactly where your heart is. The test is to reveal to you where you really are in the walk of faith. You may not be as ready as you think. Can you be obedient during this time of waiting? Are you quick to disavow, become frustrated, or disobey? Are you quick to doubt it all?

Before a harvest can come, you must prove your obedience. God is the greatest steward that ever existed. He wrote the book on it. So before He sends you on a major mission or brings in the major harvest you're expecting, He gives you the opportunity to prove yourself in the smallest areas of instruction. Why does that happen? He is being a good steward over what He's about to bring you.

Know this: *God being a good steward doesn't mean He is cheap or stingy.* He doesn't scrape the bottom of the barrel to bless you. He's not going to give you "just enough." Remember our scripture. God said in Deuteronomy that His blessings will come upon you and *overtake* you. So get that straight.

Stewardship is provided as a grooming tool, preparing and enabling you to handle the abundance. Will you do whatever He says while you're waiting?

Maybe He's instructed you to pray a certain way every morning. Perhaps He's telling you to visit the sick, the lonely, or the brokenhearted. Maybe He's told you to call a friend and encourage them during their trials. Have you made time to do these things? Or have you been too busy doing other things, such as working a job or a ministry?

We all think we have good reasons for disobeying God. You may think it will be easier if you put it off or gave it to someone else to do. It won't be. The road will be more difficult if you do that.

A Sad but True Story

There was a pastor of a very large church who employed a young man with a call on his life. This man was to move into the inner-city and live among the residents as a missionary representing the home ministry. This new missionary truly had a great heart for these inner-city people, spending much time in prayer for them.

He left his secular job and all that was familiar to him and moved on-site. He preached with great compassion to them. He and his wife established Bible studies, children's groups, and mingled one-on-one with them. Their home was open to these people twenty-four hours a day.

The pastor, though, discovered this missionary had accounting skills and he needed those skills in his office. Instead of hiring another person with the same skills, he pulled this missionary to work in the accounting office. It soon became difficult to meet the needs of the people in the inner-city. The resident missionary was now rarely "resident."

Two months later, the Lord woke this pastor in the night and told him to put the missionary back into the place of his calling. The pastor was inspired and repentant. The next day he called the missionary into his office and told him of the visitation. It was a time of great joy and vision.

Time passed, but the situation remained the same. A year after the Lord spoke to the pastor, the missionary was still inside the office doing the same accounting job. Once known for his joy and vibrancy, the missionary had now become distant and disgruntled. His ministry now had little effect on the inner-city residents. The missionary now had little respect for the integrity of the pastor and ministry that sponsored him. He fought offense and bitterness on every occasion, daily searching for his way out of that particular ministry.

Why did this happen? The pastor failed to obey the Lord. His passivity towards the Lord's instructions made his heart insensitive to the plan of God in this segment of ministry. It didn't just affect the pastor's life. The missionary was now affected and had become ineffective. The people who were to be ministered to suffered, doubting the integrity of the missionary. The community suffered, and the entire ministry missed the time of harvest in that particular area because of disobedience.

A man's ways will always seem right to him; but following his ways instead of the Lord's will always end in destruction. (See Proverbs 14:12.) If God tells you to do something, do it His way, not yours. There's a reason for it. Whether or not you understand it all; whether or not you think you have time for it, do what the Lord says to do. Obeying Him can only be for your good and the good of others.

Big Things Come in Small Packages

These types of things may seem very small to you but they are very great on the scale between "Amen" and "I've got it." Remember, what seems great on earth is not necessarily esteemed in heaven. We will be surprised at some of the things we overlooked on earth that are actually magnified in heaven.

Each time we refuse or fail to obey the Lord, our hearts grow harder. We become callused and insensitive to His Spirit and that's where the danger occurs. Before long, we've missed the timing of our harvest, or given up on it completely because of a hard, insensitive heart.

So if the Lord puts something on your heart, do it. What may seem small to you produces great obedience. It prepares and establishes a capacity within your heart to obey at any cost, at any time, doing any thing, no matter how great or how small it may seem.

Right now, I want you to check yourself. Are you feeling tired and spiritually dried up? Has the Word lost its punch? Does it seem that revelation is nowhere to be found?

I'm sure you've checked yourself for sin, but go a step further. What was the last thing God asked you to do that you have failed to do? It's probably not a big thing, or you would remember it. Whatever it was, do it! Your obedience will unclog a river of life that's been shut up by disobedience!

Begin now to obey the voice of the Lord. One minister said, "All the small things combined become the direction of our lives." Some of you need to make up for lost time. Be quick to obey Him in the things He speaks to your heart, and you'll begin to notice the gap growing smaller between "Amen" and "I've got it!"

Chapter 7
Roadblock #5: Wrong Associations

> *"Do not be so deceived and misled! Evil companionships (communion, associations) corrupt and deprave good manners and morals and character."*
> *1 Corinthians 15:33* AMP

The Beck translation of that verse says, *"Bad company ruins good habits."* Before we go any further, I want to make a point-blank statement: *Refuse to give anyone access into your life who is not in agreement with the Word of God.* You can be nice and friendly, but don't allow anyone access to your heart who doesn't know the Word.

Ungodly people can be really nice people. Yes, you read that correctly. Ungodly simply defines a person who doesn't know the Word of God. There are degrees of ungodliness and we usually imagine the worst when we hear that word. An ungodly person can be nice and polite, yet speak opinions that are not in line with the Word. That person can be sweet and thoughtful, yet be sleeping with the mate of another. I've even heard some preachers say phrases that are not scriptural.

In choosing your relationships, don't let "nice" fool you. "Nice" is not enough! When speaking of relationships, the Bible makes no references to sweetness being your guide. The Bible refers to only two classifications: godly or ungodly; light or darkness; saved or unsaved; righteous or unrighteous; saint or heathen. Every person you meet or talk to is one or the other.

You must let go of ungodly relationships if you are going to pursue the things of God. We all know people on different spiritual levels. Work and pray with the person who is making an attempt to know God and come out of ungodly opinions and lifestyles. If they continue in ungodliness and think you're the goofy one, get away from them.

I'm not talking about divorcing your husband because he has a bad attitude. Don't leave your wife because she's having a difficult time believing as you do. When your mate begins talking badly, go into the other room. If you must confront, then tell the mate you love him/her, but you know their attitude is wrong and you want peace in the house. Then hug him/her and leave the room.

You can stand for truth, but the Holy Spirit must be the One to make a change. God will honor your stand. It may be a little difficult, but hear me: Don't cave in just because someone else may doubt God.

That kind of attitude is kin to people who drop out of church and quit serving God because of hurts or hypocrites. How crazy is that? Why would you want to jeopardize your relationship with the Lord because someone else is goofed up? Your salvation wasn't based on another person and your blessings aren't either. When the set time comes, God has His way no matter what else is there!

Don't allow relationships to discourage you or to negatively influence you. Pray for your mate. Pray for your parents or in-laws. Pray for your relatives who think you're crazy. Pray for them, and God will work towards the good of it.

The Secret Place

You may be asking, "Pastor Russ, I am surrounded with ungodly people at my job. How do I escape them and their influence?"

You escape by entering into your secret place with the Lord. I'm not talking about getting up and going to a quiet place and spending time with the Lord. Many times, you can't just get up and leave the room — especially on the job. Instead, you enter into the secret place of your heart — the place where the Lord communes with you on a daily basis. You can actually escape your surroundings and worship the

Lord. The secret place is where you will find joy and peace. It's where every jabbing wound is healed.

Now you can't enter into that secret place whining, "Lord, I just got cussed out. They're going to fire me!" No! It won't work that way. There are no whiners or complainers allowed in the presence of God. You have to enter in with praise. Tell God that you are going to worship Him and enter into His peace.

Did you realize that the word "push" is an acronym for the word "pray"? **PUSH: P**ray **U**ntil **S**omething **H**appens. So push — pray — until the turmoil leaves your mind and heart. Then you'll find yourself in perfect peace even though World War III may be happening around you.

God Brings Good Friends

In Psalm 119:63, David declared of himself, *"I am a companion of all them that fear thee, and of them that keep thy precepts."* David wanted friends who loved and sought the Lord as he did. If you don't have any friends like that, ask God to bring them to you. He will.

Find friends who believe the Word as you do. You may not always agree on certain things, but the vital principles of the Word will be unanimous between you. The Bible says that a friend will sharpen the countenance of another friend as iron sharpens iron.

64

(See Proverbs 27:17.) A true and godly friend will sharpen the words of your mouth, your outlook, and your mental capacities. In other words, a godly friend accents the wholeness of God in your life.

Now you may not always like what a godly friend has to say. I've seen iron sharpening iron, and sparks fly! The two metals rubbing against each other produces a great heat. The heat bends, molds, and sharpens the iron. I may not always like what my wife has to say, but she's godly, she's my best friend, and she knows how to sharpen me. Besides all that, she's beautiful!

Enjoy life with godly people. Take good vacations and do fun things outside of going to church. God gives you friends so your life will be whole and complete. He knew you'd be strange if you were isolated, so don't be so spiritual that you can't come out among the living!

God is not against having fun. He is the God of joy. In fact, He said the joy of the Lord will be your strength. (See Nehemiah 9:10.) So find a godly friend and have a deep and hearty laugh together!

Troubles don't seem as bad when you spend time in the presence of a good friend. You may even leave with more insight and revelation into God's goodness!

Your associations can make the wait for your harvest seem shorter or longer than eternity itself. Your relationships can strengthen you during the time between "Amen" and "I've got it," or they can sow seeds to destroy everything you've believed for.

Don't allow relationships to be a roadblock on the way to your harvest. The enemy may use the ones who mean the most to deter you. Realize what's happening, pray for them, love them; but never compromise or pull back from what you're believing for.

When the time of fulfillment comes, the doubters will become believers. Let God get the glory and allow Him to work His plan. As for you, press and pursue!

Chapter 8
Roadblock #6: Broken Focus

When we first get a glimpse of what our harvest could be, we jump up, run around and dance, shouting "Amen! Hallelujah!" We're slapping everyone a high-five and feeling so energized that we could jump over a telephone pole! We are *focused*.

However, the time between "Amen" and "I've got it" soon turns into weeks and then months. We don't see even the slightest manifestation of what we've believed for. In fact, it seems like trouble abounds on every side. The rent is due, the washing machine broke down, and the car stopped for no apparent reason. It seems that every time you go to the mailbox, it's filled with bills.

You're probably amazed at how bizarre the atmosphere is around you right now. Battles and wars will come at a very high pace during this time, and those battles come to wear you down, distract you, and break your focus. In fact, people live double lives because of a broken focus. They're on fire one minute, and a smoldering coal the next.

> *"[For being as he is] a man of two*
> *minds — hesitating, dubious, irresolute*
> *— [he is] unstable and unreliable and*
> *uncertain about everything (he thinks,*
> *feels, decides)."*
>
> *James 1:8* AMP

This scripture defines broken focus. Divine, godly focus keeps you on track. It protects you from temptation, keeps your relationships on the right course, and fuels a godly fire within you. It causes you to hate sin and love God. So, of course, the goal of the enemy is to break your focus. Let's look at some of his schemes. If one of these schemes appears to be circumstantial evidence around you — identify it and kill it!

1. Giving in to persecution and pressure. If your determination isn't strengthened by the Word, then pressure and persecution will squeeze the life out of you. When the focus goes, the harvest wanes. Your passionate focus will both draw and repel people. Learn to rightly divide the two and walk right through it to the other side. Remain focused. The war is on and God has promised that the battle is His, not yours. You are not alone — God is with you. Follow Him.

2. Revelation becomes "familiar." It's important to daily ignite and strengthen what God has shown you. Keep your vision alive. The harvest you're believing for is to be considered precious and valuable. When familiarity sets in, what was precious becomes commonplace. Focus becomes unimportant and so do the results.

3. Listening to and following alternative options. Don't lose sight of the plan God gave you. When you're scattered in thought and direction, you'll lose focus. God wants an "Isaac" (a divine result) and not another "Ishmael" (a carnal result). Don't be wimpy with what God told you to do. Focused people could really care less about what others think. Stay with the plan.

Passivity = Easy Prey

As a whole, society is passive. Passivity always leads to a broken focus. The banner over the devil probably reads something like this, "Show me a passive person and I'll show you a conquered land."

Break out of that lethargic, "anything goes" attitude, and dare to be a "Godly Abnormality" in this generation! There is nothing passive or normal about God and His Glory. Therefore, there's nothing impossible about your harvest.

What you're believing for is only impossible to negative thinkers. Stay in the atmosphere where your dreams and your harvest can be seen and achieved. Associate with people of focus, watch them, and learn their ways. Then be passionate in your focus for what God has shown you.

As you go through this particular roadblock on the way to "I've got it," remember that the ones who successfully received their harvest didn't obtain it because of education, assets, upbringing, good breaks, calling, talent, or looks. They obtained their harvest because of a passionate focus.

The same is true for you. The old saying is true, "What burns on the inside shows up on the outside." *Your focus will determine the outcome of your destiny.*

Chapter 9
Roadblock #7:
Unthankfulness

Thankfulness is a spiritual force in your life. It exudes from a grateful heart, rising upwards to the throne of God. When you sow thankfulness unto God, you'll reap an incredible, never-ending supply of results.

If thankfulness is a wellspring of joy and strength, you can see how unthankfulness would be a disastrous roadblock on the way to your harvest.
If you can experience a bountiful overflow from thankfulness, then it makes sense that unthankfulness will hurl you headlong into a dry and thirsty pit! An unthankful lifestyle goes from one dead end to another. You'll never move ahead. You'll just keep hitting wall after wall, becoming more and more embittered and unthankful.

Thankfulness is more than an attitude. It's a lifestyle. It's magnetic. It draws blessings to you. The atmosphere surrounding thankfulness is rich and bountiful.

You may ask, "How can I be thankful when things are so bad? I feel so discouraged." *Thankfulness begins when you remember the good things God has done.*

Romancing Your Faith

At a time when it seems that little to nothing is happening, it's vital to focus on thankfulness. Sure, it may seem like hell is all around you — and it very well may be — but you have so much to be thankful for!

Disappointment causes us to be unthankful. You won't move ahead until you break off any disappointment that has you temporarily paralyzed. You do that by speaking out what you are thankful for.

I heard one minister comment that this is the time where so many Christians miss out on the blessings of God. In this place of waiting, the place between "Amen" and "I've got it," this minister said God wants us to "romance our faith."

But I've noticed that most Christians are defeated at this roadblock. Their harvest doesn't come as soon as they had hoped, so they act like they're frozen in a lull. They don't know what to do with the waiting time.

Disappointment and frustration sets in. Since that's their focus, then that's all that comes out of their mouths and they miss the intent that God had for them. He intended for this to be the place where they deeply fellowshipped and communed together with Him. He looks for it to be a place where we romance our faith in Him. It's a place of great thankfulness.

Participate with Him. Romance your life in God during this time. Think of your relationship and position with Him. This is the moment to remember all the good times and all the good things He has done for you. Remember how He brought you through the fire, the flood, and all of those adverse circumstances. Thank Him for always coming through for you. He even turned the bad things around for your good.

Has He spoken a word to you? This is the time to thank Him for it and confirm your love and belief in Him. Thankfulness allows your love-life to come alive and flourish!

Think of a marriage. If the couple only complained and nagged all the time, one week together would seem like a lifetime. On the other hand, if the couple compliments one another, loves one another, is joyful at the thought of the other, then a lifetime isn't long enough to live together! Why? Because the love, romance, and thankfulness for one another causes time to pass quickly. The couple didn't notice that the days had turned into years.

So it is with God. When we are thankful, each day is vital. His set time or due time for us may still be ahead, but thankfulness produces trust, security, and well-being. You'll be blessed by the little day-to-day things instead of disregarding them because the big thing hasn't come yet.

Begin to thank God for your possessions, for your family, and for your job. Thank Him for your health and the lack of sickness in your body. Thank Him because you know Him, and that your name is recorded in heaven. Look and listen for Him in every detail of life.

We, as the body of Christ, will not see the glory of God without thankfulness and love rooted in our hearts. Unthankfulness is a sin. It's prideful.

Unthankful people are enthralled with themselves, but I've never seen one of them create their own air to breathe or their own water to drink. Unthankful people are militant and demanding. The Lord said because these people refused to serve Him with joyfulness and gladness of heart (thankfulness), they would have to serve their enemies. (See Deuteronomy 28:47.)

An unthankful personality is always cranky and cutting, always creating an atmosphere of discouragement. Needless to say, they never receive the harvest that God intended.

What I've described so far is only the tip of the iceberg. Beginning in chapter one of Romans, we see how, if left unchecked, unthankful mindsets can create a lifestyle of idolatry, sexual perversion, and animalistic, carnal darkness.

> *"For although they knew God, they neither glorified him as God nor gave thanks to him, but their thinking became futile and their foolish hearts were darkened.*
>
> *Although they claimed to be wise, they became fools.*
>
> Romans 1:21-22

The quickest way to dishonor God is by being unthankful. If we're unthankful for something, we take it for granted. When something is taken for granted, we lose the knowledge of it, or its value depreciates. When a person is unthankful, they lose their knowledge of God. (See Romans 1:28.)

Praise and worship is thankfulness and is a time when God reveals more of Himself to you. When you make a choice to operate in thankfulness, three things will happen.

1. You will operate in the power of God. You imitate who you admire. You'll act like God, speak like Him, and look like Him in the earth. When you acknowledge Him as the owner of all the earth and are thankful to be His child, you'll operate like Him.

2. You will have God's provision. As I've said before, when you sow unto God, you will reap incredible results. Inside your harvest will be the seed for the next harvest.

3. You will walk in partnership with God. You will become His answer in the earth. God gives through people and He'll use you to bless others. Be a channel and not a clogged drain. Get money to give money. Money itself isn't evil, but the love of it is. See yourself as a distribution center of blessings. Blessings come to you and out they go to help others. God promotes those types of people as His partners.

Remember, there is a strong spiritual law associated with thankfulness. It not only honors God and stills the enemy, but it also consistently keeps the issues of life flowing from you to receive more and more of His Spirit and anointing. *Thankfulness is sowing unto God and one can only imagine the harvest of return!*

PART TWO

Chapter 10
Do You Know What
Time It Is?

In the first part of this book, I spoke of knowing time in a different fashion that I'm going to speak of now. I explained time as a form of patience and maturity. You'll never be able to see God move in your life in His fullness unless you understand that particular aspect of timing.

But in this chapter, I'm going to reveal the timing of God in another, very vital aspect. This phase of time will also have a tremendous influence in your life, but only if you can recognize it and understand how to operate with it.

Do you know what time it is? I'm not speaking of Pacific, Central, Mountain, or Eastern time zones. I'm talking about the dispensation of time. Webster's New World Dictionary describes dispensation as "the ordering of events under divine authority." Do you know what God is doing right now, universally, throughout the world? Do you know what He is saying to America? To the nations? To the Church?

Modern-Day Martyrs

We all remember the shootings at Columbine High School in Littleton, Colorado. Why would two young men go into a high school and kill their fellow students and teachers? Some of the students they killed were strong believers. Several students survived to report the last conversation between those murdered and those who killed.

It went something like this: With a gun pointed in their faces, the students were asked, "Do you still believe in Jesus" When they responded "Yes," the trigger was pulled and instantly those students were in eternity.

I highly honor those students and believe they were modern-day martyrs. Could you be that strong in the love of God to stand for Him in the pending pressure of death? From that day, numerous other schools have been closed for a period of time due to other plots that have been discovered. Hear me strongly: **God is speaking to America.**

When those students stared at the end of a gun, materialism meant nothing. Don't misunderstand me. I'm not saying that God doesn't want us to prosper. Prosperity is a portion of His covenant and His glory, and I'm going to talk about it in another chapter. What I am saying is that the Church must understand what time it is, and we must repent and align our hearts with the true gospel of Jesus Christ.

Don't be found focusing on self-centered, side issues. Don't be more concerned with driving a Rolls Royce than you are with the welfare and salvation of others. Be a believer. Stand for something that shows the heart of God to the nations. The world understands materialism. What they're searching for is the substance and the keys of life, and that's only found in the truth through Jesus Christ.

There's a Season for Everything

Where I live in Southern California, we don't get to experience the four seasons in a year. We have to suffer through the sunshine, low humidity, warm temperatures — maybe a little earthquake or two — year round.

However, most of America experiences spring, summer, fall, and winter to some degree or another. As long as the earth exists, there will always be night, day, and one season after another.

You can tell when the leaves begin to turn into vibrant reds, yellows, and oranges, that the fall season is near. When the leaves fall and the cold harsh winds begin to blow, winter has arrived. We all love the fragrance of spring, and the fun in the summer. I said all of that to remind you that we can tell when natural seasons change.

The spirit realm also has seasons. Ecclesiastes calls it "a time." You may have read it in some poetic form,

81

but I want to point out to you that everything the writer talks about in Ecclesiastes chapter three, has to do with a particular season in your life. Let's read it and understand it in that light.

> *"To everything there is a season, and a time for every matter or purpose under heaven.*
>
> *A time to be born and a time to die; a time to plant, and a time to pluck up what is planted.*
>
> *A time to kill, and a time to heal; a time to break down, and a time to build up;*
>
> *A time to weep, and a time to laugh; a time to mourn, and a time to dance;*
>
> *A time to cast away stones, and a time to gather stones together; a time to embrace, and a time to refrain from embracing;*
>
> *A time to get, and a time to lose; a time to keep, and a time to cast away;*
>
> *A time to rend, and a time to sew; a time to keep silence, and a time to speak;*
>
> *A time to love, and a time to hate; a time of war, and a time of peace."*
>
> *Ecclesiastes 3:1-8*

In other words, there is a spiritual timing for every purpose of God.

What Season Are You In?

I ask you once again, do you know what time it is? In reading those previous verses, do you see where you may be in your life at this moment? Do you understand why you may be in the place between "Amen" and "I've got it?" **There is a season to every purpose of God for your life.** One of the most important things we must do in that season is *rest*.

I'm not talking about resting from church or active service with the Lord. I'm talking about learning to rest in His plan, and allowing Him to work out whatever is necessary within your life.

Too many times we think we can speak our destinies and it is forced to happen that way because we spoke it. Please don't get into that error. If you do, you'll have lesson after lesson to learn until you understand that God's purpose is the one that must be fulfilled in the earth — not yours.

Are you in the season of rest? The season of launching out? The season of transition, forsaking and cutting off old ties that have kept you in bondage?

Do you know your place in this generation? Are you trying to imitate and fashion yourselves after others, or are you willing for God to groom you by His own hand? Are you still trying to be noticed by those who you think "have made it" in ministry or business?

83

Are you measuring earth's successes as heaven's approval? Or are you willing to allow God to use you and cut the path He's designed for you to follow? Allow me to ask you once again, do you know your place in this generation?

Do you know the heartbeat of God for the nations at this time? Do you know how to work and rest within this season so God can show you what He desires to show you, and work out what is necessary in your life?

No matter how old you are in the Lord, you are in a spiritual season at this moment. It's vital that you understand it and learn your role in it. If you'll do that in this place between "Amen" and "I've got it," the end results will be much stronger.

Don't Stop at the Church

Just as everything in it's natural season has the inward ability to survive and thrive in it, so you have the inward keys for the spiritual season you are presently in.

The Church is the only force on earth that has the keys to life. We are to go out into the "field," or the world, and demonstrate those keys. But you can't operate with those keys unless you know what they are and how to use them. We are a people placed strategically in this generation to proclaim the kingdom of Jesus Christ.

84

I heard a minister say that many have forgotten the work of the kingdom because they found a church. That's so true. The church building and the congregation are not a means to the end — they're only the beginning.

You have a work to do that is larger than the local church. You are here to work the kingdom of God into the earth and to reap the harvest. You are a citizen of the kingdom, not merely a member of the First Church on the Corner.

The local church is a place of training and equipping. It's there that you understand more how to use the keys you've been given. But don't stop at the altar of your local church. The power and the gifts you've been given are not to just be used behind some pulpit or to cast demons out at the altar.

The early Church knew better. Unfortunately, that's been the mentality of the present Church. Sadly, the ones who need the power and gifts you've been given aren't present. The ones who need your message aren't within the hearing distance of your pulpit, so don't stop there or think you've done your duty by preaching and going home. Don't build a little commune within the congregation and isolate yourself from the world.

As a believer or a fivefold minister, your high calling isn't based on the height of your platform or the loftiness of your pulpit. Your high calling is to reach the "field." What is the field? It's where the harvest of souls — the lost, the world, the hurting — comes from. It's where the eyes and heart of the Lord is focused upon!

Don't Wait Until It's Too Late

How sad it would be to stand before the Lord and all we could present to Him was what we did inside the church walls. At that time the truth will dawn upon us, but it'll be too late.

Did we not know His purpose? Did we not understand why we were sent? Did we not realize that we were the salt of the earth and not the salt of the church? Were we not destined to be a light in the world?

This is the time and season for us to develop the heart of God. It's the only way that we can ever manifest His glory. We'll talk about this in more detail throughout the following chapters.

A Time for True Disciples

If you're a disciple of the Lord, Sundays should be a day when you receive confirmation from what you've been studying and hearing the Lord say the other six days of the week! Each day should be a day where you go out into the world — the "field" — to sow, cultivate and reap the harvest for the Lord.

If you're a disciple instead of just a church-attendee, then you're a true believer and the Lord will use you. A disciple aligns his thoughts with the Word of God and understands that his place of waiting is really a place of strategic training for a specific encounter. You are a true believer if you know the God of the House rather than merely the house of God.

Change Our Nation!

Throughout the world, almost everyone has heard of what has been deemed the *Pensacola Revival*. Almost four million people have passed through its doors since the inception of the move. My wife and I had the privilege to visit several of the services there.

The first night we arrived at six o'clock. I was amazed to discover that since four o'clock that afternoon, three thousand people had been in the auditorium praying. Those people weren't doing the little shimmy-shimmy-bless-me prayers. They didn't have someone with a microphone, directing how they should pray, accompanied by someone playing music on the organ.

No, they were loudly groaning and travailing at the altar, in the aisles, and under the pews for those who didn't know Jesus Christ as their personal Savior. They weren't consumed with riches for themselves or what God could do for them. They were crying out to God for America to change!

87

These people knew the God of the House. They had experienced the heart of God and were responding from the supernatural touch that had changed their lives and their motives. The entire atmosphere was charged with the holiness of God. The presence of God was so strong that it could transform a life by just stepping into the place.

God wants to use you to change your home, your city and your nation. He has strategically placed you in this generation and has equipped you with the wisdom to know what to do. He has given you the spiritual strength and fortitude to stand in the face of adversity and declare the Word of the Lord. He has placed within you the heart of God to see as He sees. You can never represent the Lord in the last days unless you possess the heart of God.

I believe that you are in a strategic place between "Amen" and "I've got it." I believe it's time to analyze your spiritual position, your motives, and your purpose. I believe we are in a season of repentance, a season to rethink our priorities, a season of transition.

Will you take the challenge? Before you go on to the other chapters, will you pause and take inventory? Do you know what time it is?

Chapter 11
Character is the Issue

Character defines *who* you are and *what* you are.

Because of that fact, I'm going to go into detail on the various issues of what true character is. At times you may wonder what all I'm saying has to do with the place between "Amen" and "I've got it," but by the time you finish this chapter you will understand why character is so important and why it is a primary issue between standing or crumbling.

Simply defining yourself as a believer in Jesus Christ does not exempt you from growing and shaping the character within you. In fact, believers have many more opportunities to show their character than those who do not believe.

Show Them You're Different

I believe in letting your light shine before others. But sometimes, young believers do themselves an injustice by proclaiming their Christianity before the world, especially in the workplace.

Don't misunderstand me. I'm certainly not telling you to be a "closet Christian." I believe in radical, extreme Christianity, and standing in the face of the devil and adversity. But we need to understand that when we proclaim certain things, others automatically view us as being in a state of perfection.

Don't ever think that people aren't hungry to see Jesus Christ live and operate through you. But if the believer has not worked out character issues, then when trials and tests come, that believer might act differently than others are expecting. Before you know it, your Christian testimony is ruined. Those in the workplace just mutter, "Yeah, there's another one. He's no better off than I am." That's one reason why the media jumps to reveal a lack of character in Christian leaders and Christian people.

Tests and trials happen to everyone, believer and unbeliever alike. The difference between a Christian and those who aren't is the way the circumstance is handled. That's what the world is hungry to see. They want to see a *difference*. The world is hungry to see hope and faith fulfilled. It takes character and integrity to show that.

You're a Witness to Someone

Character is a primary substance in the place between "Amen" and "I've got it." Character sustains you when all others turn against you.

Character strengthens you when it seems that you have no friend in the world.

A man once said, "Character is what you do when no one else is looking." Do you act one way at home and another way while in the public eye? If so, how can you expect to receive anything from the Lord? God has never honored a mixture of good with evil, or a little bit of the false with the true. Whether you are known by the masses or not, you will be a witness to someone.

There are many people in my church who will never be seen by the masses. But their individual callings and giftings are vital in reaching our area for Jesus Christ. Their godly character in the midst of crisis and victory will be viewed by everyone their lives may touch.

The kingdom of God is not about one person in the limelight. It's about "whosoever will." When you stand before the Lord, His eyes will be focused on you alone. Did you fulfill what He asked you to do? When you see yourself in that light, obeying Him by buying a loaf of bread to feed a needy person is just as important as obeying Him by going to China as a missionary. The key is to obey — and to obey with the character of God.

A Slow Poison

Deception is a breeding ground in those who have not developed their character. Perhaps God is showing His mercy towards you in this place between "Amen" and "I've got it." Maybe this is a place for you to analyze your character, so let's talk about some of the pitfalls.

Lack of character is like a slow poison. At first, we may not see the end results. If we are deceived into thinking that we can continue to act without character and be okay, then the decline of sin begins.

That's how many Christian leaders fell in the days past and many more will fall in the days ahead. Sometimes Christian leaders and Christian people think they can continue to get away with sneaky little things. Before long, that lack of character begins to infect their personalities and their way of thinking. Sin has taken root. They have forgotten that God is the One who sees every little thing. They have forgotten that promotion comes from the Lord, and not from how good they've made themselves look before the people. By then, lack of character, or sin, is their lifestyle.

The Anointing is Not Character

It's a great error when we mistake the anointing of God for the character of a person. That's why many people are shocked when they discover that their minister is actually a human being with imperfections and needs much like themselves. They've only seen their minister operating under the anointing — which is God's anointing and not their own — and it's assumed the minister is perfect.

We need to understand that the Bible clearly states that the anointing turns someone "into another man." (See 1 Samuel 10:6.) In other words, when someone is under the anointing, that's the closest to perfection that we see on the earth, because God is giving a portion of Himself through that minister so others will repent, change, and be drawn to Him.

When someone operates under the anointing and flows with it, that person is not their own. Everything they do and say should be under the influence and inspiration of God. Operating in the anointing makes that person very convincing and appealing.

When people don't understand the anointing and how it operates, it causes them to focus on the leader instead of God. They think the leader is the one with all the answers and all the power, but God is who they should be pursuing.

The greater problem is when the leader begins to focus on his or her gifts and anointing more than the character of God. That's where ministries set themselves up for a great fall. God will not share the glory in what belongs to Him and Him alone. Understanding the anointing in that segment, you can see that when the anointing lifts, the minister is a human being like everyone else. That's where character comes in. Ministers must pursue the character to match their gifts.

Character and the Gifts of God

The gifts of God are given by Jesus Christ and distributed throughout the body of Christ. (See Romans 11:29 and Ephesians 4:8.) But those with gifts must be good stewards of them. Those gifts will have little influence in the earth and will be short-lived if character is not developed and exercised to carry them.

Yes, it's true that gifts are given without repentance. It's true that certain giftings in leaders will draw certain things and certain people to their ministries. However, that same gifting will destroy the leaders carrying it if character is not developed to handle the power, the persecution, the attention, and the results.

Story after devastating story has been written and told of tragic endings for those who possessed powerful giftings but refused to develop the godly character within them to administrate it.

Although God never recalls the ministry gifts He has given, many destroy their own destinies from the lack of character to carry it. They never heeded His prompting to develop their inward character to match the anointing He gave them.

Little Things Mean a Lot

I'm talking about character issues such as keeping your word, paying a bill when promised, temper tantrums, secret sex sins, power plays, dividing the brethren against one another, favoritism, gossiping, backbiting, taking the credit instead of giving it to God, pride, unteachableness, having an infallible spirit, unforgiveness, being critical and bitter, being undependable and blaming it on the leading of God, greed, the love of money/materialism, and so on. Those are a few of the character issues that must be dealt with in order to carry the anointing of God for the long haul and to reach the high calling in life.

Kenneth Hagin once said, "Payday doesn't always come on Friday." What he meant was, the end results may not always come immediately — but they will come. You will reap what you have sown, and don't ever think otherwise.

When a minister comes down from his position as leader, sets aside the opinions of people and his pressing agenda to seek the Holy Spirit on a daily basis, and lives his personal life by the Word of God, that leader will develop the character necessary to carry the anointing. The presence of God will reflect in the minister's personal life as well as in his public life.

Character and Faith

Character will affect your level of faith. If you are doing something contrary to the character of God, it will affect how you believe. It's very safe to say that our level of character will depend on our level of faith.

THE PLACE BETWEEN "AMEN" AND "I'VE GOT IT!"

If someone was described as having "great character," I would look at his lifestyle. I would look at how he handled persecution and trials. I would watch him when he believed God for something.

Faith without character is no faith at all. So if it was said that you had faith, yet demonstrated a lack of character, I would see that you had promotional Christianity, empty words, fluff without the substance, and were a person who wanted to climb the ladder of Christian politics to be seen by men.

You might be thinking, *Wow, Pastor Russ. You are really hard about that.*

No, I'm not. If we are to carry the gospel in this generation, it's time we realize what we are carrying. Christianity is not a hobby nor is it a crutch. Christianity is a lifestyle and you'd better have the strength to live it. It's easy to say "Yes," but it takes the strength of God to say "No." It takes a strong personal relationship with God to be a voice in the midst of a seared, scattered and confused generation.

I'm not talking about natural faith. Anyone can have positive thinking or natural faith in themselves and what they do. Successful businesses are built every day with natural faith and good business sense. That's why many family businesses fail when they are passed to the next generation. It's only the supernatural faith and character that is passed from generation to generation that survives.

The Early Believers Knew It

"For I say, through grace given unto me, to every man that is among you, not to think of himself more highly than he ought to think; but to think soberly, according as God hath dealt to every man the measure of faith."

Romans 12:3

The early believers understood that when Paul spoke of faith, he also spoke of character. In the early church, faith without character was immediately rebuked and dealt with. James 2:14-26 tells us that we show our faith by our works. The early believers knew that to possess true faith, one must also demonstrate the character to carry it.

One of the keys was not to think of himself more highly than he ought to think. In other words, don't think you can get away with sneaky sins, thinking God doesn't know about it. People who do that set themselves up as their own god. They are deceived into thinking that they possess the power to make something happen. Notice that Paul said, *"To every man that is among you,"* so no one is exempt from demonstrating character.

We All Have the Same Measure

Just as we were all given a measure of faith, we have all been given a measure of character. How much is your measure? It is enough to finish the course before you! However, you must cultivate it and allow the character of God to grow in your life. My friend, Roberts Liardon, once said that we all have the same muscles that Arnold Schwarzenegger has, but the difference between him and us is that he used his!

The same is true for faith and character. We all have it, but some have exercised and used theirs more than others and it shows! First Corinthians 2:16 says that we have the mind of Christ. If we have His mind, then we have His character. But just as we must renew our minds and groom our thought life to line up with the Word, we must also exercise our character to reflect His.

Character is not something that we get once and never have to exercise again. Just as physical exercise is something we must continue to do, demonstrating the character of Jesus Christ can be an hourly "exercising" adventure. Situations that present themselves will always ask the same question: *Are you going to do what is right according to the standard of God?* It doesn't matter if your day is going great or if it's the worst hour you've ever seen, you can still exercise your character to rise up within you and do what is right.

Sometimes you won't even have to think about it. You'll automatically know what is right and do it without thought, because you've established your character in that particular area. At other times, you'll have to stretch every ounce of faith within you and slap your screaming flesh to do the right thing! That is the day-to-day exercise of character.

Character Creates a Habitation

Character is integrated with the fruits of the Spirit: love, joy, peace, long-suffering, gentleness, goodness, faith, meekness, and temperance. (See Galatians 5:22-23.)

• Character is honesty, truthfulness, integrity, and doing what is right.

• Character maintains a standard of righteousness in a world without standards.

• Character never does what it feels like doing, making it's own laws between right and wrong.

• Character is based on the Word of God and His standard.

Character hurts your flesh and your carnal desires. I'm not going to sugarcoat it. As I stated before, sometimes you'll feel good after a character decision; and sometimes your flesh aches because it wanted to do something else.

Character creates the platform for the glory of God to inhabit your life and your church, and that's what we're after.

The results of a lifestyle of character will always be righteousness, joy and peace. The lack of character is satisfied with a visitation from God, but a lifestyle of character yearns for God to come and live within. People of character create an atmosphere of stability, trust, and peace.

If you find a church that is led by and filled with the character of God, you'll find a people without limits. To them, the waiting time between "Amen" and "I've got it" is a time of expectation. People of character view that waiting time as a place of training, knowing their outcome will have produced the pillars to carry the gift. They will settle for nothing less.

If You're Breathing, It's Not Too Late

One of the greatest things about the kingdom of God is that you are never too old to begin. When the majority of people in the world retire from their secular jobs, they see their lives being almost over. There are no more corporate ladders to climb, no more promotions to reach for, and no more striving to attain. God doesn't recognize that attitude, and I shudder at the thought of it. As long as you're breathing, it's never over with God.

As I'm writing this book, I've gone a great distance with God and I have no intentions of stopping or slowing down. In fact, my life will be over before I can conquer everything I foresee.

But some of you reading this book are just starting out. It's never too late to obey the Lord and follow Him. Some of you are being reserved for leadership ministry in this new century. If Jesus tarries His coming, you will be the ones to take the body of Christ to new heights and depths in the spirit. You will be responsible for the accomplishments of the Church and the nations that will be turned to Christ. If you groom yourself today, you will be the one to hear His voice and repair the places that were damaged and broken.

How will you make yourself ready?

Preparation always precedes expectation. You must prepare in the natural realm before you can accomplish anything in the spiritual realm. You must obtain within before it can manifest without. Is that the reason you find yourself in the place between "Amen" and "I've got it?"

Today you must groom yourself in moral character. Godly, moral character comes each time you choose to do the right thing when you had the chance to do something else. The young Christian martyrs at Columbine High School in Littleton, Colorado chose to do the right thing; it cost them their lives.

Reality Check

At this moment, ask yourself: *Who am I?* Go past your physical image, your intelligence IQ, and the superficial image you want others to see. Ask yourself, *Who am I, really? Am I a cookie-cutter Christian produced on a name it-claim-it assembly line? What do I really believe? Who and what is God to me? What do I stand for? What course am I following?* The decisions you have made today are showing your true character and who you really are.

The majority of the decisions we make take little thought. What we're going to eat or what we're going to wear has little influence on our character. The real test is when the stakes are high, the chips are down, and your choice might be very unpopular. Whether all eyes are on you or not, your decision at that time to do what is right and to reflect the love of God shows the fiber of character within you.

What Are You Feeding?

Not long ago, I was given a copy of a public graduation speech given by a Marine Corps Commandant General. Although he wasn't speaking to the body of Christ, I felt his words were so befitting.

His fantastic, thought-provoking speech went something like this:

"Those who can reach deep inside themselves and draw upon an inner strength fortified by strong values always carry days against those of lesser character. Moral cowards never win in war. They might believe that they are winning a few battles here and there, but their victories

are never sweet. They never stand the test of time and they never serve to inspire others.

"Those who have the courage to face up to ethical challenges in their daily lives will find that same courage can be drawn upon in times of great stress. When the test of your moral character comes, regardless of the noise and confusion around you, there will be a moment of inner silence in which you must decide what to do. Your character will be defined by your decision; it is yours and yours alone.

"When you are wrestling with a decision, consider the poem 'The Eagle and the Wolf.' When a great battle rages inside me, one side of me is a soaring eagle. Everything the eagle stands for is good, true, and beautiful. It lays its eggs on the mountaintops. The other side is a howling wolf that represents the worst in me. He eats upon my downfalls and justifies his presence in the pack. Who wins this great battle within me? The one I feed; the one I feed." Who wins the battle of character within you? The one you feed. If you feed upon the Word of God, the Word will come out from you. If you feed upon the television set and the words from the wrong associations in your life, the contrary will come from you. What goes into your heart will come out of your mouth.

Character in Proverbs

Proverbs 4 is wonderful instruction for developing character.

> *"But the path of the just is as the*
> *shining light, that shineth more and more*
> *unto the perfect day."*
> *Proverbs 4:18*

Character will keep you. It must be developed on a daily basis starting with the small issues. But when we exercise ourselves in small things, our character grows stronger and brighter with passing day.

> *"The way of the wicked is as darkness:*
> *they know not at what they stumble."*
> *Proverbs 4:19*

Those who do not know or recognize the standard of God choose their own way. They choose between what is right and wrong according to the way they feel at the moment. That double standard always produces confusion and instability. Those kinds of people can never understand why things don't go well for them.

> *"My son, attend to my words; incline*
> *thine ear to my sayings.*
> *Let them not depart from thine eyes;*
> *keep them in the midst of thine heart."*
> *Proverbs 4:20-21*

The psalmist tells us why it's so important to keep the Word of God in our hearts.

> *"For they are life unto those that find*
> *them, and health to all their flesh.*

Keep thy heart with all diligence; for
out of it are the issues of life."
                              Proverbs 4:22-23

From your heart comes all the responses to, the attitudes for, and the character of life.

> *"Put away from thee a froward*
> *mouth, and perverse lips put far from*
> *thee."*
>   Proverbs 4:24

Be careful who you listen to. Choose your friends wisely. If people refuse to change, then get away from the ones who would taint you by their language and behavior.

> *"Let thine eyes look right on, and let*
> *thine eyelids look straight ahead before*
> *thee.*
> *Ponder the path of thy feet, and let all*
> *thy ways be established."*
>   Proverbs 4:25-26

Don't look backwards. Forget the past. If you made a wrong decision, then learn from it and go on. Don't look to the left or the right. Stay focused on what God has spoken to you and on what His plan is for your life.

Consider what the Lord would have you to do in every situation that presents itself, then choose the way of godly character. That's how your ways and your lifestyle will be firmly established in the plan of God.

What are you doing with the measure of character you've been given? It just might be that your place between "Amen" and "I've got it" is a training ground of character. If you exercise your character while in this place, it will prepare you like an anchor for the situations and the ministry to come.

Don't be found like the Israelites, circling around the desert for forty years due to a lack of character. Groom yourself for the task at hand and you'll be positioned for the task ahead. In all of your waiting and in all of your getting, understand this important key: *Character is the issue.*

Chapter 12
Increase and Enlargement

Many think just because they're Christians they can ask for anything they want and God will give it to them. If you've been with God for very long, you've found out that there's more to it than that. Every scripture in the Bible that deals with receiving has a preceding qualification before it. What is that qualification? *The will of God.*

Dwell in Him

Throughout the New Testament, Jesus gives us the keys to receiving. Those keys are found in His presence. When you seek Him, you will know what to ask. When He occupies your every thought, you will want what He wants.

Let's survey some of these scriptures.

> *"For your Father knoweth what things ye have need of, before ye ask Him."*
> *Matthew 6:8*

In other words, God will supply your every need. If you think you need something and don't have it, stay in His presence. Fellowship with Him and inquire about it. Before long, you'll either have what you need or you'll discover you didn't need it as badly as you thought. You may find out that it was some wild desire that would end up getting you into trouble, such as a debt you might not want to pay.

> *"For every one that asketh receiveth; and he that seeketh findeth; and to him that knocketh it shall be opened.*
> *If ye then, being evil, know how to give good gifts unto your children, how much more shall your Father which is in heaven give good things to them that ask him?"*
> *Matthew 7:8,11*

Verse eight speaks of a personal relationship of a person who diligently inquires of the Lord, seeking the treasure He's placed in their lives for the harvest of the earth. Verse eleven ties it all in. God will give what is good for you. He doesn't give it just because you asked.

The Heart of God

For those of you who are parents, don't you follow the same rule for your children? You give them what is good for them and what they are responsible to handle and take care of. Every now and then you might give them something that was based solely on their desire, but you don't make a habit of it. Why? Because it would spoil them and corrupt their hearts. They wouldn't learn how to value what they had, and they would end up disrespecting you because of it.

Why do we think God is different? It's His example that teaches us how to be good parents!

Now stick with me, because I'm going somewhere with this. *The key to increase, enlargement, and guaranteed return is in having the heart of God.*

> *"Abide in me, and I in you. As the branch cannot bear fruit of itself, except it abide in the vine; no more can ye, except ye abide in me.*
>
> *If ye abide in me, and my words abide in you, ye shall ask what ye will, and it shall be done unto you.*
>
> *Here in is my father glorified, that ye bear much fruit; so shall ye be my disciples."*
>
> John 15: 4,7-8

Now let's read those same verses in the Amplified version.

> *"Dwell in Me, and I will dwell in you — Live in Me, and I will live in you. Just as no branch can bear fruit of itself without abiding in (being vitally united to) the*

> *vine, neither can you bear fruit unless you
> abide in Me.*
>
> *If you live in Me — abide vitally
> united to Me — and My words remain in
> you and continue to live in your hearts,
> ask whatever you will and it shall be done
> for you.*
>
> *When you bear (produce) much fruit,
> My father is honored and glorified; and
> you show and prove yourselves to be true
> followers of Mine."*
>
> John 15:4,7-8 AMP

You can see from those verses that those who receive
what they ask for dwell in the Lord. Those are the
ones who won't ask for anything contrary to His will
without being pricked to the heart because of it.
What they ask for brings glory to the Lord and
produces much fruit in the earth.

So you can see that asking for a Mercedes to keep
up with the neighbors is far from the heart of God.

Abiding and Increase

I wanted to quickly lay that foundation before I go
on with this chapter. If you're in the place between
"Amen" and "I've got it," it's imperative that you
check your heart motives. Are you dwelling with
the Lord? Are you in deep fellowship with Him, or
are you just going through the motions from what
you heard preached from some pulpit? Did you

misinterpret what you've heard another preach? If so, is your misinterpretation causing you to lose faith in God?

If you are dwelling in God, abiding in Him, your life will yield an increase. How can I say that?

> *"Yea, the Lord shall give that which is good; and our land shall yield her increase.*
> *Righteousness shall go before him; and shall set us in the way of his steps."*
> Psalm 85:12-13

God wants you to increase, and He wants to steer that increase with His righteousness.

What Does It Mean?

Take a look at the Hebrew interpretation for the word "increase." Strong's Exhaustive Concordance states that the word means produce; i.e., a crop or wealth; bring (forth), carry, lead (forth) [# 2981, 2986].

Webster's New World Dictionary defines the word "enlargement" as to make larger, expand, to become larger. An example would be to turn a photograph that was a five by seven into an eight by ten. In other words, increase it to the next size.

It's God's will for you to go up! Even if you are down and out, abased, or feeling like you're in the dregs of life, God wants you to go up! So, take heart. Even in the natural we have to prune a tree or cut back the branches so it will produce more fruit in the coming season!

Those who grow roses certainly know what I'm talking about. Every Fall, the branches of the rose bush is cut back. Why? If not, the long green stems wouldn't be able to support the weight of the rose when Spring comes. Pruning the bush enables the plant to bush out and produce beautiful roses when the time comes.

Just as in the natural, if you're in the place between "Amen" and "I've got it," you must position yourself for increase and enlargement. If you are dwelling with the Lord and abiding in His vine, your place of waiting is going to give way to increase and enlargement!

This principle is for every area of your life; not just the area of finances. God wants you to have abundance. He wants wealth for you, but He wants your heart in position so you'll know what to do with it. He wants to see a return come to you.

It doesn't matter what kind of negative report you get. It doesn't matter what people say about you or to you. God wants increase and enlargement for you life.

Misplaced Treasure

God doesn't want you caught up in money. He doesn't want money to be your treasure. He wants your treasure to be in heaven and your life on earth to be caught up in Him.

Remember the rich young ruler in Mark 10? He approached the Lord and asked what he had to do to go to heaven. Jesus answered him by rehearsing the commandments.

The rich young ruler said, "Yes, I've done those things from my youth." Then, in verse 21, Jesus looked at him and loved him, saying, "But one thing you haven't done. Sell all that you have and give it to the poor, and you will have treasure in heaven. Then take up your cross and follow Me." The Bible says that when the rich young ruler heard that, he was very sad and went away grieved.

Why? Because he trusted in his great riches more than he could trust in the Lord. He was so rich that he couldn't imagine giving it all away and following the Lord. He didn't have a deep, abiding relationship with God. If he did, he would have heeded the voice of the Lord, realizing that if he forsook all and followed Him, he would have been richer than he'd ever known. His riches might have come in other ways or God might have given him ten times more than he previously had.

I don't know the plan of God for this man's life. But we can see that he trusted in his wealth more than he trusted in God. Great possessions owned him instead of him owning them.

It's Still the Same

Jesus is still presenting the same plan. As the rich young ruler walked away, Jesus turned to His disciples and said, "How hard it is for them that trust in riches to enter into the kingdom of God." He didn't say we couldn't have riches. He didn't say we couldn't have nice things or that we were supposed to be poor. He didn't say we weren't supposed to have money in the bank.

No. Jesus said that the one thing that would keep us from having the God-kind of life on earth is trusting in riches. Or, you could say that the one thing that keeps people from knowing the abundance of God, is trusting in a source other than Him. It all goes back to the heart issue.

Back to the Heart

I don't know how you've heard it preached, but God is going to bring wealth into His Church. It's part of His plan. But there is a heart issue that's involved with it. Part of that issue is to have the heart of God within us manifested in such a degree that we desire the benefit of others to be above our own. Maybe that's what He's working in you right now, as you wait in that place between "Amen" and "I've got it." You'll never increase or enlarge in any area without the heart of God within you.

I believe that wealth is coming to the Church, and I believe it's for the Great Harvest. But until it comes in its fullness, there will be every twist of doctrine and utterance preached along those lines.

It's like every other thing that God was about to do in times past. People would get an unction of what was coming, and many times they would put their own understanding to it and preach it that way. That's where scriptural error and excess always crept into the body of Christ.

As we matured into whatever God was doing at the time, we had to repent from our excess and error and align our hearts with what He was really doing and saying. Many have become so materialistic that they actually think their personal wealth is a sign of the favor of God. We've just seen that it wasn't true in the case of the rich young ruler. The favor of God begins with the condition of your heart. You can confess favor until you're blue in the face, but until your heart is circumcised, your words will produce little.

Prosperity isn't isolated to money. Prosperity means an increase and enlargement in every area of your life. Are you content with your life, married or single? Are you healthy or working towards it and seeing improvement? Is there peace in your mind

115

when you lay down to sleep at night? Is there enough money to pay your bills? Is there joy in your house? Those are just a few of the ways to measure prosperity in your life.

The Heart of a Leader

Think for just a moment about the great leaders of God.

Moses was once a man with great wealth as a prince in Egypt, but he forsook it all to find God on the backside of the desert. He realized wealth was not the essence of true life. Moses had a heart that hungered after God. As a result, there is no price that could purchase what he did. He set a nation free from the clutches of hell itself. To this very day, that nation worships God in their own land.

David was just a shepherd boy, chosen by God to be the king of Israel. Though he grew to become one of the richest men in all of history and the greatest king in Israel's history, the secret to his success was said by the prophet Samuel, *"The Lord hath sought him a man after his own heart" (1 Samuel 13:14).*

In his day, Abraham was one of the richest men in the known world. Yet he heard the voice of the Lord, picked up everything he owned and headed out, looking for a city built by God. He never thought to trust in his riches. Because the example of his heart was so turned towards the Lord, Abraham is called the father of our faith.

116

Joseph had a dream from God, yet that vision caused him years of trauma. Whether he lived as a slave in Egypt or as a mistreated prisoner in the darkest confines, Joseph never turned his heart from the Lord. As a result, the favor of the Lord was greatly upon him, and eventually positioned him as second in line to Pharaoh and all of Egypt.

Paul knew how to abound and how to abase. Once a very wealthy college boy, he was taught by the greatest of the Pharisees. But one experience on the way to Damascus changed his heart forever. He separated himself for three and a half years in the Arabian desert, seeking and hungering after the Lord.

When Paul returned to churches in the book of Acts, his revelation of what happened from the cross to the glory causes us to know Jesus Christ in a greater way. The issue was the heart.

Where is your heart as you wait in the place between "Amen" and "I've got it?" Some people stand and believe God for about ninety days. When they don't see a harvest or an increase, they quit. As I've stated before, we have to position ourselves for increase and enlargement.

Give, Work, Obey

Picture an apple tree. The increase of that apple tree would be an apple. From the seed of that apple, another tree would be produced and so on. Before you know it, you'd have an entire orchard.

You have to see yourself producing something. Give, work, be faithful, and obey. Position yourself for increase.

You can take a seed out of an apple and look at that tiny brown thing in your hand. It doesn't look like an apple tree. It doesn't look capable of producing a limitless amount of fruit. But it has the ability and potential to do it. You can't just stand there, holding that seed, confessing over it to be an apple tree.

No, you have to position the seed for increase and enlargement. You have to plant the seed, water it, fertilize it, weed it, anchor it when strong winds blow, spray it with pesticides, protect it if a frost comes, prune it, and cultivate it. If you are diligent to do those things, that tiny brown seed will be capable of endless possibilities.

Why are we any different with ourselves? Position yourself for what you are believing for. Plant the seed of God's Word deeply in the good soil of your heart. Water it, fertilize it by the Spirit, and weed it from the evils that rise up to choke your dream.

When the strong winds of controversy and persecution blow against you, position yourself with extra strength from the Word and from prayer. When the cold, hard times come and threaten to abort your position, cover yourself with extra doses of the Word and counsel from godly friends. Allow the Spirit of God to prune your life so it will yield a bountiful return.

Position Yourself

Position yourself and start standing against your enemy of unbelief, of doubt, and of debt. Refuse to conform to the pressure coming against you. Mark 11 says to speak to the mountain — the overwhelming problem — and tell it to be removed and cast into the sea.

Water has always been symbolic of the Spirit and the things of God. So to me, the "sea" would represent a vast circumference of the promises of God. So the next time your mountainous problems loom against you, position yourself with the heart of God and pronounce judgment against those problems by casting the care of them into the promise and peace of God. If you'll do those things and not grow weary, you'll see increase and enlargement.

Chapter 13
Guaranteed Return

Don't let the title of this chapter fool you.

First of all, let me state that God is not some slot-machine, and secondly, remember this central truth: *You are not guaranteed anything and everything you ask for.*

You may be asking, "Pastor Russ, you sound like you're contradicting yourself." No, I'm not. If those sentences I've just stated shake your doctrine — good. If you believe you can haphazardly ask for anything and get it, you need to be shook up!

As we established in the previous chapter, a guaranteed return is much like increase and enlargement. It is based upon abiding in the Lord. When we abide or dwell in His presence, then what we ask for will be in the plan of God and will come to pass. Some answers come immediately; some take time. When the guaranteed return of God takes time, it puts you in the middle of that place I call between the "Amen" and "I've got it."

Zoe Life

To me, the word "guaranteed" means to stand good for, to secure or endorse something. Jesus Christ stated His purpose in the earth in John 10.

> *"The thief comes only in order that he may steal and may kill and may destroy. I came that they may have and enjoy life, and have it in abundance — to the full, till it overflows."*
>
> John 10:10 AMP

Read that verse again. Notice that Jesus stated that He came so we would have enjoyment of life in abundance.

In my studies, I have found that Jesus intended for us to have life that was superior in quality and nature. That life, or *zoe* life, means salvation, health, healing, deliverance, prosperity, peace of mind, and peace of soul. He guaranteed that life for us by His death on the cross of Calvary, His obtaining the keys to death, hell, and the grave, His resurrection from the dead, and His glorification at the right hand of the Father in heaven.

If that *zoe* life is a guarantee, then you can turn the tables on the negative report from the doctor. You don't have to lose your mind. You don't have to have a nervous breakdown. You don't have to go bankrupt. You don't have to believe you have multiple personalities. You can be delivered! You don't have to sing about the sweet by and by; you can enjoy life right here, right now!

It Doesn't Matter What it Looks Like

A guaranteed return is going to come to those who are following Jesus Christ — His disciples — and to those who believe His promises.

The apostle Paul wrote the majority of the New Testament. He was the one who instructed us on how to live in those promises and to stand for them. He was boiled in oil, stoned in Lystra, put in jail most of his life, left for dead on a city street, bitten by a poisonous viper, and nearly wrecked at sea from a violent storm. If he called all those circumstances "light afflictions," I would hate to see the heavy ones!

Paul knew something about the *zoe* life of God and the guaranteed return of it in his life. He knew how to tap into the peace of God despite the circumstances. He understood that no matter the conflict, the promises of God were guaranteed for his life.

I want you to understand that no matter what it looks like, no matter how difficult your life may be at the present time, the promises of God are guaranteed for you if you'll believe for them. No one ever said it would be easy. No one ever said you would go through this life without trials, troubles, and testings. But God did promise a way through it if you diligently seek Him.

More Than Willing

If you're in the place between "Amen" and "I've got it," you have some decisions to make. If you shouted "Amen!" then you believe God has promised you something and you're reaching for it. If your guaranteed return hasn't come as quickly as you thought it would, then take each day one day at a time, expecting a fresh word from the Lord. I want to give you some keys to remember while you're waiting for the guaranteed return.

"If ye be willing and obedient, ye shall eat of the good of the land."
Isaiah 1:19

The first thing I want you to do is make sure you're willing to do whatever the Lord tells you. Some people are willing but they stop right there. You may hear them shouting in church, "I'm willing, Lord, I'm willing! Send me, I'm willing." But they continue to sit on their blessed assurances and never go any further. Ten years from now, they're "still willing," but nothing further has happened.

We can be willing, but that's only half of it. There's a conjunction in the verse we just read, so let's read it again.

"If ye be willing AND obedient, ye shall eat of the good of the land."
Isaiah 1:19

124

The other word connected in that statement is "obedient." If you're willing and God tells you to do something, follow through and make the picture complete — be obedient.

One reason God branded King David with the banner, "a man after my own heart," was that David followed through to do the perfect will of God. Yes, he made mistakes. Praise God, that gives us hope! But the key to the heart of God is that a person be willing and obedient.

Let's say you got all excited about God, so you said, "I'll do whatever You tell me, Lord. I'm willing." So He answers and tells you to give all the money you have in your wallet in the offering. Now you're shocked! What? You think, *All of my money? How can I go to lunch with the group? Do I have enough gas in my car to make it home?* Then you start shaking your head, *I don't think that was God. I think I just got excited.*

You only lived up to half of it. You won't eat of the good of the land, the increase, the enlargement, or the guaranteed return. It was wonderful that you were willing, but God wants you to go all the way and be obedient! Understand that God is trying to put money into your hands, not take it away from you.

The sooner we understand that obedience brings blessing, the sooner we'll walk in it and cross over into "I've got it!"

A Little Twist

Now let me turn a little twist here. *When you are obedient, remain willing.* Some people get so mad that they have to follow through and be obedient, that they lose their blessing. Oh they may give their money, or buy something for someone, but they grumble and complain the entire time.

There's no blessing in that kind of obedience. Remember the conjunction, the combination: *willing and obedient!*

In your quest to be willing and obedient, don't argue with the Lord. You may think that you know it all in a particular area. In fact, you may be an expert in that field. But God may tell you to do it differently. If you know He's spoken to you, do what He says.

One of My Favorites

The Bible has a great story about a professional that the Lord corrected.

> *"And it came to pass, that, as the people pressed upon him to hear the Word of God, he stood by the lake of Gennesaret,*
> *And saw two ships standing by the lake: but the fishermen were gone out of them, and were washing their nets.*
> *And he entered into one of the ships, which was Simon's, and prayed him that*

*he would thrust out a little from the land.
And he sat down, and taught the people
out of the ship.*

*Now when he had left speaking, he
said unto Simon, Launch out into the deep,
and let down your nets for a draught.*

*And Simon answering said unto him,
Master, we have toiled all the night, and
have taken nothing: nevertheless at thy
word I will let down the net.*

*And when they had this done, they
inclosed a great multitude of fishes: and
their net brake.*

*And they beckoned unto their
partners, which were in the other ship, that
they should come and help them. And they
came, and filled both the ships, so that they
began to sink."*

Luke 5:1-7

I love this story. I can just see this crew that Simon
Peter was with. When I was in the Navy, every time
I took leave and went ashore, there was always a
crew of commercial fishermen. Let me tell you,
sailors knew some words, but these guys — they
knew some words! They were rough and tough with
beards and unshaven faces. I mean, these were men's
men. They had tattoos every place you could see,
and "I dare you" was their middle name. They were
like the cartoon character, Bluto — the one who
always tried to fight Popeye and cause him trouble.

Commercial fishermen in Jesus' day were just as rough and tough. Jesus didn't walk up to them and say, "Hey guys, that's a nice net on the side of your boat. Would you like to be a part of My group?" No! Jesus was strongly anointed and He knew how to present the plan. It was a set-up, for the whole time that Peter was washing out his nets, Jesus was preaching from his boat. Peter was forced to listen to the entire sermon.

When Jesus finished preaching, He turned to Peter and said, "Go back out into the deep and let down your nets for the catch of your life."

Now I'm not a fisherman but my son-in-law is. And from his experiences, I know that you don't fish in the heat of the day. If you do, the sun will cast your shadow on the waters and the fish will see you. Once they see you, they'll go anywhere but to your net.

So here was Jesus, telling this rough and tough group of commercial fishermen to go back out in the heat of the day and let down their nets for a huge catch! Can you imagine how outrageous that was!

Notice that Jesus didn't *ask* Simon Peter to do it, He *told* him to go back out. Don't try to tell me that Jesus was like that ridiculous picture that we see painted of Him, looking anorexic carrying a sheep under His arm! Jesus was a muscular, buff carpenter — his tools weren't electric. He did carpentry by His own muscle and human strength. Jesus was also a man's man!

A Real Man

Sometimes, if you're not willing and obedient to do the foolish, you'll never get the miraculous. Peter, sweaty and tired, looked up and said, "Lord, we've been working all night. But here it is — nevertheless, at Thy word I will let down the net." That's what I call a real man.

Peter's net was so filled with fish that the boat started to tip. The net was breaking, so he had to call others to help him pull it all in. Another ship came to the rescue and both ships were so filled with fish that they started to sink.

> *"When Simon Peter saw it, he fell down at Jesus' knees, saying, Depart from me; for I am a sinful man, O Lord.*
> *For he was astonished, and all that were with him, at the draught of the fishes which they had taken.*
> *And Jesus said unto Simon, Fear not; from henceforth thou shalt catch men."*
> Luke 5:8-10

Jesus is so cool. There He was, smiling and teaching rough and tough Peter a lesson about partnership. If the Church would understand about partnership with God, there wouldn't be an empty seat in the house. The world would be overrun by hungry, spirit-filled believers who knew and understood the power of God and the heart of God.

Obedience Guarantees Promotion

Peter was willing and obedient, so he ate from the good of the land. He received a guaranteed return. But notice that his willing obedience gave him a promotion as well. The abundance of fish prospered Peter, but it wasn't about prosperity. It was about the souls of men. Peter was now ready to be a fisher of mankind, drawing and pulling them into the kingdom of God.

Guaranteed return is all about obedience. It's all about the willingness to do what God has spoken to you to do. The Holy Spirit may stop you one day and say, "Go over there and witness to that man; witness to that business woman. That person is hurting. You may not see it, but I do. Can I use you to tell them about the peace through Me? Will you be a partner with Me in the end-time harvest?"

If you're in the place between "Amen" and "I've got it," make it an exciting time. Get your eyes off yourself. Get hungry for the Lord. Seek to hear Him, then obey what He says. Life can be extremely exciting if you will willingly obey the Lord today!

Chapter 14
Progressive Abundance

Not everyone reading this book is believing for finances. But for those of you who are, this chapter is for you. Even though I'm writing on the subject of money, I believe you can apply this chapter to anything you're believing for. Don't stereotype this chapter and don't skip over it.

As long as we're in this world, we will need money to implement the divine will of God in our lives. Somewhere, some way, money will be involved in His plan for your life. So right now, whether you're believing for money or not, sooner or later you will need more of it. Sometime in your life, believing for finances will be your place between the "Amen" and "I've got it."

If you've been a Christian for any length of time, you'll hear a lot about the promises of God. But are we "wearing" those promises? Are those promises visible in your life?

You may answer, "Well, Jesus Christ is in me, Pastor Russ." Yes, He's in you, but is His abundance visible in your life? It's my desire for you to manifest the abundance that God has for you.

A Vision of Progression

In Ezekiel 47, the prophet Ezekiel was shown a vision from the Lord. When the Lord takes you out in the spirit, He's going to show you something strategic that will benefit your life. Your vision is not going to be the sight of fat baby angels floating on clouds and eating grapes.

No, a true vision from the Lord will change your life. In this vision, it was as if the prophet was looking down at the Church, or the Body of Christ. Ezekiel was a type and shadow of Christ. From it, the Lord continues to teach the Church a very valuable principle in manifesting the abundance He has for each of us.

> *"Afterward he brought me again unto the door of the house; and, behold, waters issued out from under the threshold of the house eastward: for the forefront of the house stood toward the east, and the waters came down from under from the right side of the house, at the south side of the altar."*
> *Ezekiel 47:1*

Remember that "water" has always represented the Spirit of God.

"Then brought he me out of the way of the gate northward, and led me about the way without unto the outer gate by the way that looketh eastward; and, behold, there ran out waters on the right side.

And when the man that had the line in his hand went forth eastward, he measured a thousand cubits, and he brought me through the waters; the waters were to the ankles.

Again he measured a thousand, and brought me through the waters; the waters were to the knees. Again he measured a thousand, and brought me through; the waters were to the loins."

Ezekiel 47:2-4

It's Not an Overnight Thing

Can you see what the Lord was showing Ezekiel? First, the waters were to his ankles. Then He measured again and the waters came to his knees.

We need to understand that we won't go from poverty to extreme riches overnight. To think otherwise is rarely the will of God, unless years of a foundation has already been laid. You'll be ankle deep with God before you're knee deep. From time to time, you may get out into the spirit and be over your head, but you won't keep that anointing in your life on a day-to-day basis unless you've learned how to walk ankle deep.

That's an important principle for you to remember in the place between "Amen" and "I've got it." God measures what is due you according to the depth of the spirit that you live in. He wants to solidly grow you into full maturity, and that only comes one step at a time. So make sure that you're not believing for something over your head if you're only ankle deep with the things of God.

> *"Afterward he measured a thousand; and it was a river that I could not pass over: for the waters were risen, waters to swim in, a river that could not be passed over."*
>
> *Ezekiel 47:5*

Have You Seen It?

Now we'll see what happens when we live and abide in the Spirit of God over our heads, or in other words, doing His will and not our own at all times.

> *"And he said unto me, Son of man, hast thou seen this? Then he brought me, and caused me to return to the brink of the river.*
>
> *Now when I had returned, behold, at the bank of the river were very many trees on the one side and on the other.*
>
> *Then he said unto me, These waters issue out toward the east country, and go down into the desert, and go into the sea:*

which being brought forth into the sea, the waters shall be healed.

And it shall come to pass, that every thing that liveth, which moveth, whithersoever the rivers shall come, shall live: and there shall be a very great multitude of fish, because these waters shall come thither: for they shall be healed; and every thing shall live whither the river cometh."

Ezekiel 47:6-9

I pray that the scriptures we've just read will more than bring inspiration to you. Allow it to bring revelation to you. Ezekiel was showing us a progressive move of God. He began ankle deep, then knee deep, then progressed to the place where he was over his head, totally submerged in the Spirit and will of God!

It's Only by the Spirit of God

As you wait for finances to manifest in the place between "Amen" and "I've got it," understand that the only way you can prosper and live in abundance is by the Holy Spirit.

Throughout the Bible, the Lord tells us that we must separate ourselves from the world's system and get into the system of God. How do we see the riches of God? How do we manifest abundance in every area of our lives? How does it come upon us? By getting into the water of the Holy Spirit and allowing the Spirit of God to permeate you and live in you. Quit trying to do it the world's way and start doing it God's way.

Analyze where you are in your thinking. Are you allowing God to take you, one step at a time, into obtaining the finances that you need? If so, it should be an exciting adventure!

People go to school for years and years to become accomplished in their goals. Those students don't mind the progressive steps because they know each course they pass leads them closer to the result. Why should we be any different with the things of God?

Your place between "Amen" and "I've got it" is a school of the spirit and a school of character. It also has a timing for graduation. So don't be a drop out. Study to finish the course and show yourself approved. Understand that the move of God in your life is *progressive*.

Be a tither, that is, giving ten percent of all your increase. Give to others as they have a need and you have the means — especially to those in the household of God. If the Spirit of God tells you to invest your money in a certain place, do it. If He tells you to save, do it.

The world's system wants you to lie, cheat, make up stories, or connive your way into money. It screams at you to "Buy! Buy!" But God's system is the opposite. If He's your source, you don't need to lie and scratch your way into a raise. If He tells you not to buy something, no matter how much you want it, pass it by.

I've heard of several stories when someone wanted a particular item, and God told them to wait — but they bought it anyway. A week or so later, someone had the very same item and wanted to give it to the person. Because the person jumped ahead of God, they spent unnecessary money that could have contributed to abundance in another area.

Where's the River?

We've just read where the Lord asked Ezekiel, *"Son of man, hast thou seen this?" (Ezekiel 47:6)*. Now I'm asking you, *Can you see with the eyes of the Spirit the abundance that's waiting for you as you progressively walk with Him? Are you learning to love Him with all your heart, with all your mind, and with all your being?*

The verses we've just read state that when we progressively walk with the Lord to the extent that we are in the "river" over our heads, then healing, deliverance, salvation, and prosperity will come in some degree to every person we come in contact with!

"He who believes in Me — who
cleaves to and trusts in and relies on Me
— as the Scripture has said, Out from his

> *innermost being springs and rivers of
> living water shall flow."*
>
> *John 7:38* AMP

God didn't say that streams would flow from you.
He didn't say it was a mist. No, it's going to be a
river that will come up out of your being to manifest
the abundance of God. Can you see it? It's not about
you. It's about what God wants to do through you.
When you truly understand that concept, you can
find joy in the midst of every situation and
circumstance.

Need-Minded or Seed-Minded?

God has His system of prosperity and it's the only
system that never fails.

> *"For my thoughts are not your
> thoughts, neither are your ways my ways,
> saith the Lord.*
> *For as the heavens are higher than the
> earth, so are my ways higher than your
> ways, and my thoughts than your
> thoughts."*
>
> *Isaiah 55:8-9*

Our thoughts are usually need-minded. But God's
thoughts are seed-minded. God wants you to be a
giver.

You might be moaning, "But Pastor Russ, I don't have much of anything to give. That's why I'm believing for finances to begin with!"

Give what you can! Start out small, give it in faith to the Lord, and He will increase it!

> *"Now he that ministereth seed to the sower both minister bread for your food, and multiply your seed sown, and increase the fruits of your righteousness."*
> 2 Corinthians 9:10

You are the sower — the giver. God will give you something to sow. If you will obey Him in it, He will not only supply your need through it, but He will also increase or multiply what He gave you, and you'll increase in righteousness because of it!

Wow! With a promise like that, how can you lose?

Here's my surprise translation. I like to study all the different versions of a verse, put them all together, and create my own translation from them. I've put together the Living Translation, the Moffat, Knox, and Taylor translations of that verse for you and here's how I read it: *"For the One who made the seed will in fact give you more and more seed to plant and will make it grow so that you can give away more and more from your harvest."*

Isn't that good? You can see why God is seed-minded. Inside of that seed is your seed for the harvest. But when you're only need-minded, you cut yourself short and stop right there at your need. Think like God thinks! If He lives within you, then let Him out!

Don't Despise Where You Are

Coupled with the vision of Ezekiel and the verses we've just studied, you can understand that God's system is progressive. You start out ankle deep, giving what you have. Then when some harvest comes, you don't hoard it up or consume it all upon yourself. No, you must think like God thinks. You must come out of the world's system and get into God's system.

Take some of that harvest, listen to the Lord and trust Him, then you sow some more. Soon you'll find yourself knee deep. Continue to abide in Him, listen, and obey Him, and that river of His Spirit will flood out of you into the nations. You'll be part of the last day harvest of souls.

Don't despise small beginnings. Don't get frustrated in this place, this "school" between the "Amen" and "I've got it." Learn to work it and grow from it. If you'll follow God's plan, you'll demonstrate His glory in this generation.

Chapter 15
Oh, The Glory!

Do you know the purpose of the glory of God? We talk about it, sing about it, preach about it, yearn for it, desire for our churches to be filled with it; but would you know the glory of God if it came?

Money and Glory

Yes, the glory of God is the presence of God. But I'm going to make a shocking statement: Money has everything to do with the glory. Now don't put this book down!

One day I was studying the different concordances, and I discovered that money, finances, and abundance is spoken throughout the scriptures more than heaven is. Why? Because in heaven we won't need money, finances, and abundance! We need those things while we're in the earth, and the Bible is our manual for life on earth.

Many of us don't want to take a hard look at those subjects because the law of religion has contained us, tainted us, and kept us from God's best. We need to break out of that containment mentality! As we read in the last chapter, the waters of the Spirit, the river of God, can't be contained. God wants to enlarge and increase you.

There's A Remnant

Isaiah 10 talks about the remnant of God — those who will depend upon Him and His system and who will break out of religious and worldly confinement.

> *"He who believes in Me — who cleaves to and trusts in and relies on Me — as the Scripture has said, Out from his innermost being springs and rivers of living water shall flow."*
> *John 7:38 AMP*

Another word for "innermost being" is heart. You can know the promises of God all day long. But if His promises are not in your heart, they're just empty words. You can put a scripture over your religious unbelief or your trust in the world's system, but it won't do you any good.

We need to go past confessing the promises and begin to experience the promises, and it all starts in the heart! We'll only experience the promises as we cleave to Him.

The Glory is Physical

God wants you to manifest His glory in the earth. But the glory isn't some warm fuzzy. I hear person after person who speak of the glory as if it's a goose bump or some mystical vapor that creeps into the room. People speak of the glory like they spoke of the Holy Spirit years ago, like He was some mysterious "it" that you had to tiptoe around.

No. The glory of God is a physical manifestation, not a spiritual one. If you're in the place between "Amen" and "I've got it," then He wants to teach you about His glory so you can manifest it. He's ready for you to obtain a solid, physical manifestation of His glory. Stop jumping up yelling "I've got it!," when you're settling instead for some shallow manifestation of what He really has for you.

> *"[Even] now I rejoice in the midst of my sufferings on your behalf. And in my own person I am making up whatever is still lacking and remains to be completed [on our part] of Christ's afflictions, for the sake of His body, which is the church.*
> *"In it I became a minister in accordance with the divine stewardship which was entrusted to me for you — as its object and for your benefit — to make the Word of God fully known [among you]."*
>
> Colossians 1:24-25 AMP

143

When Paul wrote this, he must have been in the place between "Amen" and "I've got it" too!

I want to point out that in that *place*, God made Paul a steward. That's what God is trying to get through to us as well. He's trying to move us from being just a "tither" and transforming us into a "steward." It's more than just a duty. God wants to make you a steward over His glory and His abundance. He's allowing us that privilege while we're on the earth.

> *"The mystery of which was hidden for ages and generations (from angels and men), but is now revealed to His holy people (the saints),*
> *To whom God was pleased to make known how great for the Gentiles are the riches of the glory of this mystery, which is, Christ within and among you the hope of [realizing] the glory."*
> Colossians 1:26-27 AMP

Riches Mean Riches

Those who oppose prosperity from God like to quote the above verse by saying that the "riches" a Christian can have is Christ within them. Their statement is true, but it's only a half truth if you stop there. Strong's Exhaustive Concordance clarifies the Greek interpretation for the word "riches" is wealth, fullness, money, possessions, and abundance [#4149].

In other words, it pleases God to bestow on the Gentiles wealth, fullness, money, possessions, and abundance as He dwells within them for this one purpose: so the earth can witness the hope in His glory.

From that verse alone, we can see that the glory of God is physical. God wants His tangible glory to be seen throughout the earth, but it's going to come through a people who know the treasure of His presence within them. It's going to come through those who abide in Him, cleave to Him, and who are operating in His system instead of the world's system. And you have to groom your heart to participate, because the pull of the world is such a strong counterfeit.

It's Not Automatic

Let me make a very important statement here. God's not going to give you riches and abundance just because you are a Christian. No, it's going to come to those who have invested their lives to be a steward of His glory.

If you don't know how to love another, how to be real, or how to have a heart like God that sees like He sees, His divine glory is not going to be manifested through your life. God's not going to give you wealth for it to overtake and own you. God gives wealth to those who know and understand how to implement it back into the earth for the harvest.

As I've stated before, don't be so shallow to think God is a slot machine or a sugar daddy. Don't join a church thinking you'll get rich. Don't be a Christian because you think it's a life of wealth. God's picture is a lot larger than that, and He has a plan for the last day generation.

You must make the transition if you want to be a part of it. That may be one of the reasons you're in the place between "Amen" and "I've got it." It's a time of understanding and transition.

The Earth Will be Filled With the Glory

God wants people — nations — to see hope in the glory of God on your life. His glory should be in you, on you, around you. You should strive for the place where you wear the glory and anointing of the Lord on your life.

> *"But [the time is coming when] the earth shall be filled with the knowledge of the glory of the Lord, as the waters cover the sea."*
>
> *Habakkuk 2:14* AMP

I believe we're in that time. I believe it's the day when those who make the transition will be filled with the knowledge of what the glory really is.

Get Up!

What are you doing in your place between the "Amen" and "I've got it?" Are you trying to operate your life as you did before you entered this place? Are you still slapping scriptures over your hurting emotions, refusing to change attitudes and your old way of thinking? Isaiah 60 commands this generation to arise!

> *"Arise [from the depression and prostration in which circumstances have kept you; rise to a new life]! Shine — be radiant with the glory of the Lord; for your light is come, and the glory of the Lord has risen upon you!"*
>
> Isaiah 60:1 AMP

Can you believe that even back in the Old Testament that outward circumstances still depressed and paralyzed people? These verses literally means that your hour has come.

So get up, get knowledge, then give out the light and glory of God! God created you for this hour. Now it's your responsibility to learn what your role is within it.

Change your posture and your position. People should know that something is different about you. They should stop and stare at you when you go into a restaurant or walk into a room. The world may not know what to call it, but they're hungry to see the glory of God. When they look, don't act isolated or elite.

Be the salt of the earth and the light of the world. Change the lives around you. Give out what was given to you. As believers washed by the blood of Jesus and filled with the Spirit, we shouldn't be just running the race, we should be setting the pace!

Change Your Position

In Mark 2, Jesus was preaching the Word inside of a home in Capernaum. So many people crowded the place that there was no more room for anyone. A man who had palsy wanted to hear Jesus at the hope of being healed. Seeing that there was no more room inside, his friends cut a hole in the roof and lowered his bed into the room where Jesus was.

When the Lord saw their faith, He looked at the man and told him that his sins were forgiven. In other words, we're to put away any sense of guilt and walk in wholeness. Of course, the religious Pharisees, who knew the Word more than they lived it, were appalled by His statement. They didn't know who they were dealing with.

Jesus heard their thoughts and spoke them aloud. He asked the crowd if it was easier to say that someone's sins were forgiven, or to actually tell them to get up from the bed and walk. So, to show everyone that He was the Son of God, He told the man to "Arise." Immediately, the man got up from his bed and walked out of the house totally healed.

What Jesus actually told the man to do was to change his position. He was saying, "Listen, you could be standing up, but you haven't changed your position."

He's saying the same thing to us today. The Lord is saying, "When you change your posture and position regarding your role in this generation and your place in My glory, then I'm going to invade your life by showing My posture, My thoughts, and My position towards you."

Nothing Can Stop You

That's what He was saying in Isaiah 60, long before Mark 2 occurred.

> *"For behold, darkness shall cover the earth, and dense darkness all peoples, but the Lord shall arise upon you, [O Jerusalem], and His glory shall be seen on you."*
>
> *Isaiah 60:2 AMP*

That verse doesn't say that the sun goes away or that God turns the light off. No, that verse is talking about hard times and gross sin. Dark times may come, but the Lord is going to change His position regarding you. When you choose to change your posture in the midst of the darkness and get up on the inside, God's going to get up on the outside. Manifested abundance and the glory of God is going to cover you and your household.

Physical Glory in a Natural World

We've just read in Isaiah chapter sixty that the glory of God will be seen upon you. The glory has to be seen. Please hear me. That mystical vapor that some call the extent of the glory is never seen by the world. How could God get honor from that? His heart is to harvest the souls of the world!

> *"But the natural man receiveth not the things of the Spirit of God: for they are foolishness unto him: neither can he know them, because they are spiritually discerned."*
>
> *1 Corinthians 2:14*

This is why the glory must be physically seen by the lost. They can't see anything spiritually because they're not born-again. We as believers, must spiritually discern all things, understand how the glory works, and how it is to be manifested upon our lives so the world can physically detect it. If the glory was just a spiritual thing, sinners couldn't see it and the harvest of the earth wouldn't be reaped.

Remember the Vision

Remember, the glory of God in our lives is progressive. We're ankle deep, moving along, and walking in it. We're tithing, giving offerings, and giving what the Lord instructs us to do. The light afflictions come upon us — we're shaking them off left and right because we know our purpose, and nothing is going to distract us or detain us.

Then we're knee deep — giving more and listening to the Lord. Then we're up to our waist — doing more than we've ever done, and it's pure joy to do it. Before long, His manifested abundance is upon us, and we're over our heads in the river of life.

Glory and Goodness

There's a beautiful story in Exodus 33 that tells of a conversation between Moses and the Lord. Moses realized that he would be no different from anyone else in the earth unless the presence of the Lord was with him. The glory separates you and makes others take notice.

But then, an interesting thing happened between the two. Moses passionately begged the Lord, asking to see His glory. How did the Lord respond? He said, "I'll show you my goodness." (See Exodus 33:19.)

The glory of the Lord is the goodness of God. If people can't see the goodness of God through your life, they haven't seen the glory. If others can't see grace and obtain mercy from you, they haven't seen the Lord through your life.

Some people look like they've swallowed a prune, yet say they're a Christian. Others commit adultery and betray their mates, yet never miss a church service and preach to others how they should attend. The list goes on and on.

Let the glory of God be evident to others. The goodness of God through your life draws unbelievers to Him, and believers closer to Him.

The Hope of Goodness

Colossians 1:27 tells us that Christ in us is the hope of glory. Strong's Concordance interprets the word "hope" as anticipate with pleasure, confidence, and expectation [#1680].

Those words describe the anticipation of good. The glory is the goodness of God. In the midst of darkness and corruption, goodness is something the world longs to see. If you'll allow Him to manifest that goodness upon and through you, the world will see their hope. They will see the nature and manifestation of God in their midst.

Chapter 16
Fishing On the
Wrong Side of the Boat

"Spring Valley, California? Are You sure You don't mean Grass Valley, Lord?"

Barbara and I were between our first and second year of Bible school. The teachers at Rhema had taught us to wait until we had completed the full two-year program before praying about what God was calling us to do. I wasn't trying to be disobedient, but I felt like the Lord was leading me to begin praying about where He wanted us to go after graduation. During my morning shower the words, "Spring Valley, California" had unexpectedly come up from within my spirit.

Hmm, I don't see it, I said to myself as I sat at our kitchen table with a road atlas open before me, "There's a Spring Valley in Connecticut, Vermont, and Michigan, but I don't see a Spring Valley in California. Lord, maybe You mean…"

Suddenly, the words "Spring Valley" jumped out at me.

"Here it is...it's a suburb of San Diego! "

I was overjoyed to find it! The fact that Spring Valley, California existed meant that I was hearing God correctly.

Barbara was back in El Paso at the time. Her mother had passed away shortly after we completed our first year of Bible school and we had flown there for the funeral. After the funeral, I flew back to Tulsa to take care of our two dogs and our house, but Barbara stayed behind to be an emotional support to her father for a few weeks. I was anxious to tell her what the Lord had spoken to me, so I phoned her immediately.

"Honey, I believe I know where the Lord wants us to go after graduation!" I announced excitedly.

"Where?"

"Spring Valley, California. It's a suburb of San Diego."

"Well, let's obey Him, " she said with surprising simplicity.

Barbara was never one to pull any punches. If what I was hearing wasn't of God, she would know it, and she wouldn't be afraid to say so either. She had an immediate witness in her spirit when I said the words, "Spring Valley" so she joined her faith with mine.

Spying Out the Land

In March of 1989, Barbara and I decided to fly to Spring Valley for three days to spy out the land. We were scheduled to board a flight in Tulsa and change planes in Denver, Colorado for the final leg of the trip. As we boarded our connecting flight in Denver, my wife spotted a sharp looking couple boarding the plane with us.

"We need to find out who those people are," she said, "they have that 'ministerial look.'"

"You're right," I concurred.

As we settled into our assigned seats, we found that we were only three rows behind this couple.
"If I hear them talk about anything that has to do with church or religion," I said speaking discreetly into my wife's ear, "I'll get up and introduce myself."

Sure enough, about fifteen or twenty minutes into the flight, I heard the man say something about evangelism. Barbara and I looked over at each other realizing that this was our "cue." At that exact moment, the man seated on the aisle next to this couple stood up and relocated to a seat in the back of the plane. It was almost as though an angel had tapped him on the shoulder and told him to move. I immediately made my way towards the open aisle seat and sat down.

"Excuse me," I interrupted politely, "I heard you say something about evangelism. What do you both do?"

"Have you ever heard of Happy Church in Denver?" the man answered with a life-filled tone in his voice that only a born-again believer could project.

"Sure!" I said, "Everybody has heard of Happy Church—it's pastored by Wally and Marilyn Hickey, right?"

"Yeah — my wife and I are the music directors there. We're going to San Diego for a music symposium."

"Praise the Lord!"

"What are you going to San Diego for?" he asked me.

"Well, my wife and I are Bible school students at Rhema. We believe God has called us to pastor a church in the San Diego area after we graduate so we're going to spy out the land."

"It's interesting you say that," he said, "Wally and Marilyn are looking to add another pastoral couple to their full-time staff. They're looking for someone to oversee pastoral care, hospital visitation, and counseling. You and your wife would be *ideal* for the position. You should contact them. They'd ordain you, put you on a salary immediately, and offer you a nice housing allowance. You would be perfect!"

This man didn't know us from Adam and yet he was offering us a ministry position that any newly graduating Bible school student would quickly jump upon. Nevertheless, we had heard from the Lord and He had said nothing about freezing like a popsicle in Denver.

"That sounds great and all, but I have to obey what's in my 'knower.' The Holy Spirit spoke to my wife and I about Spring Valley, California. Besides that, it would have to be God because I don't like cold weather!"

We laughed.

"Well, if you change your mind," he said as he handed me his business card, "call me when you graduate. You'd fill the slot perfectly."

The offer was definitely tempting, but we had to follow what the Lord had laid on our hearts. We had no idea, however, that this one encounter would later become the key to finding our destiny.

No "Springs" in Spring Valley

After our flight landed in San Diego, we drove out to Spring Valley and found that there wasn't any spring and there wasn't any valley! It was an arid climate spiritually and naturally, much like West Texas.

We spent the first few days walking around the area and praying in tongues. We went to the town hall and post office, and we walked around in the shopping centers hoping the Lord would speak to us or send someone to say, "Thus says the Lord, you're the ones I have chosen to deliver this place!" But after two-and-a-half days of walking and praying, nothing had happened. As our three-day excursion was coming to a close, our faith was beginning to wane.

"How is this all going to come together, Lord?" we prayed in desperation.

It wasn't long before our natural reasoning began to take over. Some of the teachers at Rhema had said, "When you graduate, we don't want you to become a reproach to the Lord or to this school. Don't sit around waiting for the Lord to put you into ministry. Either go back and work for the church you came from or go out and look for a job."

With that in mind, I said to Barbara, "Now that we know we're called here after graduation, I'm going to have to find a job. You know, maybe I could go into real estate. In real estate we would have a lot of time on our hands — we could open our home and have a Bible study. That's how a lot of churches have been birthed. We could meet in our home until we have about fifteen people, then we could move to a game room at an apartment complex. Then, when we outgrow that, we can go on to a hotel ballroom."

That was my natural mind trying to figure everything out. The Holy Spirit took advantage of it nonetheless.

Late in the afternoon on the final day of our trip, we were riding down a main thoroughfare in Spring Valley when we noticed a beautiful two-story building with a Spanish style roof made of red-tile. On the top of the building was perched a sign that read, "Century 21 Real Estate." It was an extremely large facility. As we drove by, I began to sense an inner "leaping" in my belly.

"You know, I think we need to go in there tomorrow before we leave," I said to Barbara, "I sense there's something there."

"I Have Seen You On Television!"

We returned bright and early the next morning and went in to meet the owners.

"Oh, he and his wife are out of town today," one of the workers said to us, "they work with a man named Brother Andrew bringing Bibles into China, Russia, and places like that. They're board members on Brother Andrew's ministry staff."

I knew it! The owners were Christians! What were the chances of us walking into a Christian-owned business by accident? *This must be a divine connection!* I thought. Our faith level suddenly rose a few degrees.

"I'm the vice president of sales," the man continued, "Can I help you with anything?"

"Well," I said, "we'd like to meet the owners because we would like to find out about getting our real estate license and going to work for you."

"Well, at least one of you is going to have to get an eight-to-five job," the man explained. "It's going to take a while for you to get your license and build a clientele."

This man continued talking to us for about twenty minutes or so. The more he talked, the more discouraged we became. By the time he finished talking to us, our "faith tank" was almost empty.

As we walked down the front stairs to leave this beautiful two story building, we ran into one of the sales account executives. She stopped, looked straight into my eyes and said, "I know you! I've seen you on television!"

"You haven't seen me on TV," I answered.

"What do you do?"

"My wife and I go to Bible school in Tulsa."

Without warning, she grabbed me by the coat lapel and led me and Barbara into her office.

"Now I know why I'm here today," she exclaimed excitedly. "Have you ever heard of Pastor Bob Tilton?"

"Well yeah, we're from Texas originally — everyone's heard of Bob Tilton."

"Well, he has his main office here now. I'm one of the phone counselors for his ministry. Normally I'm at his headquarters on my days off, but today they ran reruns so they didn't need me. A little while ago, I felt the Holy Spirit lead me to come back to my office. I believe I was supposed to meet you."

Our faith level shot back up a few degrees.

We shared our vision with her and explained that we believed we were called to move to the area after we graduated.

"Oh, you need to get to know Paul Young. He has an office upstairs. He's a strong Christian who works for Brother Andrew. The only problem is he and his wife Karen are out of town right now."

"We were told."

"He would be excited to hear about your vision." She continued, "He's been praying with a group of people and calling for ministers like yourselves to come here by the leading of the Spirit and help the area. There are too many religious folks who come here politically, trying to make a name for themselves. You should try to correspond with him when he returns."

"I think we'll do that," I responded.

Our Faith Wavers Because Of Money

After returning to Tulsa to finish out our final school semester, we began to communicate with Paul Young and his wife, Karen. Paul told us that he and his wife traveled all over California, Arizona, and Nevada sharing Brother Andrew's vision. When we shared our dream to move to Spring Valley and pastor a church, he seemed genuinely interested.

"Look, if you come here," he said, "I can't promise you work, but I'll introduce you to some people in the area."

Paul's offer was helpful, but it wasn't exactly comforting as our severance money was beginning to run low.

After graduating in May of 1989, our faith began to waver again. According to this world's system, everything is predicated by money, and the abundant river of supply that once was flowing through our life seemed like it was about to run dry. Barbara's father knew about our financial situation and kindly offered to help.

"Why don't you just move back here and get all that religion out of your system. I'll build you a home in the pecan orchard. You can live here and Russell can get a job."

With nothing solid approaching on the horizon for us financially, we reluctantly packed everything up and moved back to Texas to live with Barbara's father.

At least we're closer to Spring Valley, we thought.

Despite our financial situation, we didn't entirely break focus. We were still believing for God to open a way for us to enter our "promised land." I dusted off my resume' and began to make contact with some of the people I knew before Bible school. I wanted to get the word out that I was looking for work. It felt miserable, but at least I was making an effort.

Everyday, after searching for work with no success, I would come home, lay on the floor prostrate and cry out to God.

"I know you have called us, Lord! I know I heard the words Spring Valley, California. I just don't know how we're going to get there!"

Everyday, Barbara's dad was asking her, "Did he get a job yet?"

I was feeling tremendous friction and the pressure was mounting.

I Can't Take Anymore of This!

After a few weeks, I finally made contact with a firm in El Paso that was looking for a marketing director. I went on two interviews and they wanted me to come in for a third. On the day of my third interview I had to reschedule because of an unexpected obligation. When I came home for dinner that night and shared what had happened with the family, my wife's father misunderstood me. He thought I had turned the job down. He became so angry he almost jumped over the dinner table to choke me!

"I can't believe how stupid you are!" he yelled at the top of his lungs.

When I looked at his face, I knew instantly that this was not going to work out. I had to get my family to Spring Valley as soon as possible.

That night, we called a friend of ours from El Paso named Audrey Weatherly. She was a real prayer warrior.

"Audrey, we've been here six weeks and we're miserable. I want you to pray for us. We're supposed to be in Spring Valley but we don't know anyone there."

"Sure, no problem," she said.

It wasn't ten minutes later when the phone rang. It was Audrey.

"Do you remember Diane Shlutz from El Paso?"

"Yes."

"Well her sister and her husband live in Lemon Grove, California. It's a little town right on the border of Spring Valley. They've got a four bedroom home there they rent for nine months out of the year to foreign exchange students. I called them and they said you could stay there this summer if you want to."

"Praise God, that's perfect!" I exclaimed.

God was making a way.

You're Fishing on the Wrong Side of the Boat!

On August 8, 1989, I packed my Honda with everything I could fit and left for Spring Valley with a thousand dollars in my pocket. I was determined to secure an income so I could set up a home base there for my wife and daughter. I felt like Abraham leaving the familiar to go to the unfamiliar.

Within two days, I arrived in San Diego with my faith in high gear. I was determined to get a job a quickly as possible. I began visiting all the employment agencies I could find in the yellow pages.

"Well, you're marketable," the job search agents told me. "You've got great skills, but it's going to take at least ninety days to find you a job."

"I don't have six days," I told them.

For the next three weeks, I faithfully looked for employment but ran into "brick walls" everywhere I turned. My faith was wavering. Day after day, the battle dragged on.

The situation was growing more desperate by the hour. My youngest daughter, Christy, was back in El Paso with her mother. Barbara's father was putting pressure on us to enroll Christy in a public school. It was early August, and by law, Christy had to be enrolled by September, or we could get in trouble with the state of Texas. On top of that, my money was running thin. I had to find employment quickly or I was going to put my family in a real pickle. I tried everything I could think of. I even put in applications at trucking companies, but the more I pushed for a job, the harder the "plowing" became.

During this time, I had been going to breakfast and lunch a few times a week with Paul Young, the man who worked for Brother Andrew. On the third week of my floundering job search, Paul took me to lunch on a Friday afternoon and said that he and his wife, Karen, had been praying for me and the Lord had given Karen a scripture concerning my situation.

> *"And he said unto them, 'Cast the net on the right side of the ship, and ye shall find.' They cast therefore, and now they were not able to draw it for the multitude of fishes."*
>
> *John 21:6*

"Tell Russell that he's fishing on the wrong side of the boat," Karen said. "Tell him to cast his net on the right side of the boat."

"Would you like to interpret that for me please?" I asked Paul with a chuckle.

"You know, Russell," Paul said with a serious tone as we were finishing up our breakfast, "you need to entertain the possibility that you didn't hear God correctly."

"Yeah, I guess you're right," I answered.

"Next Monday, I have arranged for us to have breakfast with a couple who started a small church in the area a little over five years ago. Their names are Pat and Sharon Mahoney. They're originally from Wally and Marilyn Hickey's church in Denver."

"Oh yeah, I'm familiar with Wally and Marilyn Hickey," I said.

"Two other pastoral couples from the area will be joining us too. I'll come by and pick you up Monday morning and then we'll meet them all at this couple's church. I think meeting with these pastors can give you some insight into what is going on here. We're just going to pray, counsel and talk over the possibility that you "missed" the Lord."

"Alright," I said hesitantly. But little was I to know, that just three days later, during that very breakfast, I would find out exactly how accurate Karen's prophetic word was.

Unexpected Reactions

When Monday morning arrived, Paul and Karen picked me up and we drove to Pat and Sharon Mahoney's church to meet them for breakfast. Their church was in an industrial park. In fact, it didn't look at all like a church. It had pews, a stage, and a couple of microphones, but that's about it. A sign above the pulpit read: Seedtime and Harvest Family Church.

I like that name, I thought.

Pat and Sharon Mahoney were extremely cordial, we hit it off immediately. They showed me around their building while we were waiting for the other couples to arrive. One of the couples we were waiting for was Tom and Linda Riley, who had worked as comptrollers for Jim Zirkle's ministry, Living Water Teaching. Along with Tom and Linda Riley, there were two other couples from the area who were in ministry.

When the others arrived, Pat and Sharon invited me to ride with them to the restaurant. It was a ten or fifteen minute ride so it afforded us reasonable time to talk.

"So how did you get here, Russell?" Pat asked as he turned the steering wheel to make a right turn onto the thoroughfare.

I proceeded to tell them the story of how God had supernaturally led me to Spring Valley. They seemed unusually interested in the details of how I had arrived there. When I was finished sharing, they told me that they used to work for Wally and Marilyn Hickey.

"You know, it's kind of funny you mention Wally and Marilyn," I politely interrupted, "In March of this year, we met a couple on our plane trip here who said they were the worship leaders at Wally and Marilyn Hickey's church. They tried to recruit us. They said that Wally and Marilyn were looking for someone to oversee pastoral care, hospital visitation, and counseling. We turned them down though because we felt the Lord was calling us to a work here."

Suddenly, Sharon began crying and flipping through the pages of her Bible.

I felt slightly uncomfortable, like when someone tells a joke and no one gets the punch line.

169

"What's going on? Are you alright?" I asked her, a bit perplexed by her strange reaction to my story.

"She's okay," her husband said, "We'll tell you about it later when we get to the restaurant."

No One Gives You Anything for Free!

We pulled into the parking lot of Alie's Restaurant in San Diego and made our way in to find a seat. A waitress pushed a couple of tables together so we could all sit together. I felt a bit apprehensive as we settled into our seats — almost as if I was about to go on trial. After we each ordered our breakfast, Pat began to address my situation.

"Well anyone who knows me knows that I don't beat around the bush — I get right to the point. A year ago this month," he said, "we had two credible prophetic ministries come to our church. They came through on two different occasions and spoke almost identical words of prophecy over us. They said that God was finished with this phase of our ministry and that He was going to be putting us into a support type position, under a major ministry. They also said that it would be a promotion for us.

The Lord revealed that He was going to send a stranger to take the work that we started and bring it to the next level. No one knows this yet, but Wally and Marilyn Hickey called us recently and offered us the very position the couple you met on the plane offered you. That's why my wife was crying when you were telling us your testimony in the car."

Suddenly the pieces of the puzzle began to fall into place in my mind.

"I was praying last evening," Pat continued, "because I needed to know if the Lord wanted me to close the church down or if I should turn it over to someone else. The Lord told me to turn to Ezra 5:8 where it says, *"And the work of God will go on quickly and prosper."* Then the Lord said, 'You will give the church to the stranger you meet tomorrow.'"

"That stranger is you," Pat said pointing straight at me.

I was stunned! I couldn't believe what I was hearing. All the blood suddenly drained from my face!

"No one gives you anything for free!" I heard myself say.

"No, this is God," Pat retorted with great conviction. Just then, Sharon began quoting scriptures from Amos and Ruth and sharing why she felt the Lord had directed them to give me their church. As Pat and Sharon were speaking, a look of amazement came over the faces of everyone seated at the table. They hadn't told anyone about what the Lord had been saying to them. Paul and Karen almost fell off their chairs when they heard it!

Suddenly, I felt hesitant about the speed of what was transpiring.

"I want this to be right," I said, "because we're credible people. We preach what we believe. We don't do or say something in hype and expect everyone to follow suit. The problem with this whole offer is that it's not in Spring Valley. The Lord spoke to us about Spring Valley."

"No, it's not Spring Valley," Pat agreed, "but the connection with Paul and Karen *was* in Spring Valley. They live and work there. Paul connected you to us, which connected you to your destiny! You are the ones who are supposed to be taking our church to the next level!"

"Well, I don't know," I responded trying to slow the whole process down.

"This is like the story of Elijah and Elisha," Pat continued.

"But I didn't see this vision."

"No, but a vision is transferable," he said, "Elijah transferred his mantle, or you could say 'his vision' to Elisha, and Elisha did all the supernatural works that Elijah did. In fact, his miracles were greater and more credible than Elijah's!"

I felt the presence of God, but I still wasn't sure about everything that was unfolding.

"Well I'm going to go pray, and then I'm going to call my pastor."

"Who's your pastor?" they asked.

"Charles Nieman, in El Paso, Texas."

"I've heard of him. I'd like to call him too so I can verify that you are who you say you are."

"No problem."

The Big Decision

I spent the rest of the day walking and praying along the sidewalks of the Mission Bay beach front. I really wanted to make sure I was following the Lord's plan. The more I prayed the better I felt about it, but I wanted to be sure everything was right.

At about eight o'clock that night, I decided to phone Pastor Charles at home on his private line. He was a straight shooter. I knew that if there was anything wrong with this picture, he could see it and he would tell me the truth.

"Pastor Charles, I want to ask you something, because I covet your counsel. I met some pastors today who have a congregation of about 130 people. They want to turn their church over to me. I'm not sure what to do."

"I don't know Russell, look at the books," he said, "make sure they're not in the red."

I hadn't thought of that, so I went to inspect the books the following morning. I was encouraged to find that they had a substantial amount of money in the bank and that they didn't owe anything except for a copy machine. Everything was on the level — these folks were extremely credible.

After another short season of prayer, I called Pastor Pat back and said, "Yes, I believe this is God. We'll take the church."

Pat and his wife rejoiced!

A Time Of Rejoicing

When I phoned home that night, I felt like my spirit was doing backflips on the inside of me! I was bubbling over with the joy of the Lord!

"Honey, we have just inherited a church!"

"You're kidding!" she shouted.

"Nope! And guess what? We'll both be getting a salary immediately!"

"Are you sure?"

"Yes! That's what Pat and Sharon said today. They haven't told the church board yet or even their two daughters. They're going to fly you here tomorrow for an emergency board meeting. Pack your stuff honey — you're coming to California!"

The Board Votes Us In

The board set us in as the new pastors of Seedtime and Harvest Family Church on September 6, 1989, and thanks to a visit from Pastor Wally Hickey, the congregation joyfully accepted the change of leadership. We only lost a few families in the changeover and it wasn't long before our church was experiencing steady growth.

Today, God is fulfilling His prophetic promise. He is using us to take the church to a new level of glory and revelation just like He said He would. Today, we have about 380 tithing church members who are "head over heels" in love with Jesus. We have a strong missions thrust and we're making an eternal impact on our community as well as on the nations of the world.

Don't Give Up!

Barbara and I have had hundreds of opportunities to get "hung up" by the different *roadblocks* I mentioned throughout this book. I wanted to share our story to encourage you to keep pressing for the mark of the high call in Christ Jesus. We went through many temptations and battles before we entered our promised land, but we didn't give up! We fought the good fight of faith and we endured hardship as good soldiers of Jesus Christ! That's how we got to where we are today. We refused to stop and set up camp in the place between "Amen" and "I've got it!"

Chapter 17
You've Got It — Go Get It!

> *"The Lord is good to those who
> hopefully and expectantly wait for Him,
> to those who seek Him — inquire of and
> for Him, and require Him [by right of
> necessity and on the authority of God's
> word]."*
>
> Lamentation 3:25 AMP

I wanted to close this book with the scripture that we began chapter two with. As you read it again, I believe it will take on a whole new meaning for you. The Lord is good; He's not bad, and He's not mean. He's especially good to those who wait hopefully and expectantly for Him.

God is not your problem. Your life is not your problem. Your wife or your husband is not a devil. Your kids are not demons. None of those things are your problems! But there is something out there that wants to stop you from moving into your harvest, and I believe we've labeled seven of your vilest enemies: criticism, words of doubt, walking backwards, disobedience, wrong associations, broken focus, and unthankfulness.

As believers in this end-time generation, we must be valiant in our pursuit of God and skillful with the spiritual equipment He's given us. "Waiting" is part of our character. God is a God of patience.

When Adam turned his will against God and fell from his spiritual position, God could have restored everything in an instant. I'm sure Satan laughed at God's lack of action, but God had a plan for all of humankind. He wanted a huge family in the glorious Church, and that would take patience and time. God knows how to wait for the set time.

As His children, the same attribute is built within us. We know how to wait; and when the blinders are off our eyes concerning the enemy, we know how to skillfully hurdle all his roadblocks and ditches.

I exhort you to be strong and vigilant in the pursuit of what He has promised you. Your set time — your due time — is surely coming. Train as a good soldier, fit for the Master's use. Determine, at any cost, to complete the course before you.

Right now, lift up your voice and call for God. Repent of any roadblock that has delayed your course. Change your attitude and correct your focus. Ask Him to restore you in strength and direction and to restore lost time.

If you do this, you'll be different than when you picked up this book. You'll be stronger than you were before and you won't fall for the same evil gimmicks. This time, you're going to go through to the other side and remain intact!

So take it on! Walk in your rightful position. You've got it — go after what belongs to you! Be strong in the Lord, and do great exploits in the name of Jesus Christ.

There's a place waiting for you, and I can see your name on it. It's called, "I've got it!"

About The Author

Pastor Russell Plilar is a tremendous teacher of God's Word. The message Russell delivers to his local community and throughout the world brings reformation, hope, and restoration to the body of Christ, and causes positive change in the lives he ministers to.

Pastor Russell's desire to see lives changed has caused him to reach out beyond his local Body of Believers to go to the nations where God has opened doors that no man can shut. His travels include China, Russia, India, New Zealand, and many European, Scandinavian, and Eastern Block countries.

Russell is a graduate of Rhema Bible Training Center, and is currently on the teaching staff at Spirit Life Bible College (Roberts Liardon Ministries) in Irvine, California.

You may contact him at:
Russell Plilar
c/o Seedtime and Harvest Ministries
P. O. Box 270635
San Diego, California 92198-2635
(858) 576-1622 Phone
(858) 576-7389 Fax
Webpage: www.seedtime.org
Email: rplilar@seedtime.org

To Have Pastor Russ or Barbara Speak At Your Church, Contact:

**Seedtime & Harvest
Ministries
P.O. Box 270635
San Diego, California
92198-2635**

Barbara Plilar co-pastors with her husband at Seedtime & Harvest Church located in San Diego, California. She is a graduate of Rhema Bible Training Center, and is currently on the teaching staff at Spirit Life Bible College (Roberts Liardon Ministries) in Irvine, California.

Pastor Barbara has been on fire for the Lord ever since God's healing power raised her out of a hospital bed in 1979. She is a woman of strong faith who refuses to compromise the Word of God. Barbara has purposed to reach her local community and the nations with the truth of God's Word.

Barbara is well known as a strong preacher and teacher of God's Word. Through her bold ministry many are set free from bondages, sicknesses, poverty, depression, and all manner of demonic influence. As she preaches, the traditions of men make the Word of God of no effect – are pulled down.

Barbara is a frequent minister at women's conferences locally and nationally. She and her husband have minis-tered at several crusades, and their travels have included India, China, Russia, and many other countries in Europe and Scandinavia.

Project Love San Diego

Project "Love San Diego" is a community outreach program of Seedtime & Harvest Church. The primary focus of this program is to recognize and identify needs in our San Diego Communities and to work to develop and provide solutions to those needs. The goal of project love San Diego is to make the San Diego area a better place to live by improving the overall quality of life.

On November 22, 1998, Project Love San Diego gave away 700 free turkeys as well as food supplements to communities of San Diego. During the two hours of distribution, 400 families were given bags of food. This first event was a huge success and we have decided to make this an annual event during the Thanksgiving holiday. The number of people attending this occasion was more than 1,000.

Project "Love San Diego" was a tremendous success!

To be a part of: Project Love San Diego and to Contribute to Helping The Less Fortunate, write:

"Project Love San Diego"
c/o Seedtime & Harvest
Ministries
P. O. Box 270635
San Diego, CA
92198-2635

Let Us Agree With You In Prayer Concerning Your Needs!

The Scripture states in Matthew 18:18-19, that if any two agree in the name of Jesus, your prayer will be heard.

CLIP & MAIL

_____
_____
_____
_____
_____
_____
_____
_____
_____
_____
_____
_____
_____

Name _____
Address _____
City _____ State_____ Zip_____
Phone (____) _____

Clip and mail to: Seedtime & Harvest Ministries
P.O. Box 270635
San Diego, CA 92198-2635

FRESH FIRE
Praise & Worship Team

When you strike a match, *fire ignites.* Fresh Fire is a musical group called to touch the people of God with powerful music.

Their goal is to declare and proclaim the name of Jesus and touch people with the high praises of God.

Fresh fire always strives to develop new and exciting songs to inspire God's people and bless the Lord.

Pastor Barbara Plilar

FRESH FIRE MUSIC MINISTRIES
Mission Statement

❖ **ENLIGHTEN**
Educating those called into the ministry of music through building a spiritual foundation according to the scriptures.

❖ **DEMONSTRATE**
Showing how music is an important aspect of the Kingdom of God.

❖ **IMPART**
Spiritual input through teaching, preaching and example

Contact us if you are interested in having the FRESH FIRE PRAISE AND WORSHIP TEAM minister in your church or organization.

Or, if you are looking for a church home where you can receive the uncompromising Word of God while making a difference in the lives of others, come visit us at Seedtime & Harvest Church in beautiful San Diego, California.

HORN of TRUTH

Is a tool to promote Jesus Christ as Lord and Savior and a prophetic voice giving the Word of the Lord to the Body of Christ.

TRUTH will bring freedom and clarity from deceit and falseness. TRUTH will bring freedom and clarity from deceit and falseness.

HORN OF TRUTH will guarantee to bring prophetic messages for the spiritual season we are now in, give you updates of what God is doing within the ministry, and teaching you how to be obedient with character & integrity and to fulfill the plan of God for your life.

"And you shall know the truth, and the truth shall make you free." (John 8:32 NKJV)

To Order "The Horn Of Truth" And To Be On Our Mailing List, Please Write:

Seedtime & Harvest Ministries
P. O. Box 270635
San Diego, CA
92198-2635

Topics:
- ❖ **Fulfilling the Vision**
- ❖ **Our Authority and God's Power**
  by guest Minister Bobbie Jean Merck
- ❖ **Deception**
  written by Pastor Barbara Plilar
- ❖ **The Stumbling Blocks of Iniquity,**
  written by Pastor Russell Plilar
- ❖ **Prophetic Music in the Church Today**
- ❖ **Experiencing the Fire**
  with Generation Xcellence Youth!

"Ten Year Anniversary Conference"

See the exciting teachings from our week long Ten Year Anniversary Celebration.

Speakers included:

- ❖ Juanita Bynum
- ❖ Charles Nieman
- ❖ Brian Zahnd
- ❖ Roberts Liardon
- ❖ Dr. Ed Dufresne
- ❖ John Bevere

CLIP & MAIL

10YRCOL	**Entire 8 video tape series** *(includes FREE Oral Roberts video while supplies last)*	**$100**
10YRJB1	**Juanita Bynum** *Video tape 1*	**$20**
10YRJB2	**Juanita Bynum** *Video tape 2*	**$20**
10YRCN	**Charles Nieman** *1 video tape*	**$20**
10YRBZ	**Brian Zahnd** *1 video tape*	**$20**
10YRRL	**Roberts Liardon** *1 video tape*	**$20**
10YRED	**Dr. Ed Dufresne** *1 video tape*	**$20**
10YRBV1	**John Bevere** *Video tape 1*	**$20**
10YRBV2	**John Bevere** *Video tape 2*	**$20**

Total _____